QUICKBOOKS ONLINE FOR BEGINNERS

The Most Updated Illustrated Guide to
QBO. Unlock Practical Tools, Automation
Secrets, and Industry-Specific Strategies
to Go from Zero to Pro Fast

NATALIE WARREN

TABLE OF CONTENTS

Book 1. QuickBooks Online Basics

CHAPTER 1

CHAPTER 2

CHAPTER 3

Book 2. Intermediate Tools and Features

Book 3. Advanced Features and Troubleshooting

INTRODUCTION

Welcome to **"QuickBooks Online for Beginners: [3 Books in 1]"**, your ultimate guide to mastering one of the most powerful tools for managing your small business finances. Whether you're new to bookkeeping or looking to enhance your QuickBooks Online skills, this book is tailored to help you achieve financial clarity and efficiency.

QuickBooks Online is more than just software—it's a solution designed to simplify and streamline your financial management tasks, giving you more time to focus on what matters most: growing your business. As a small business owner, you know the importance of staying organized, accurate, and informed. This book walks you through the essential tools and techniques needed to take control of your finances, reduce stress, and unlock opportunities for growth.

This 3-in-1 bundle is structured to ensure you gain a solid foundation, advance your skills, and explore professional-level features. It's designed for readers like you—ambitious, resourceful, and ready to invest in mastering a tool that can transform your business operations.

Let's begin your journey from beginner to pro, ensuring you feel confident, empowered, and fully equipped to navigate QuickBooks Online with ease.

Why QuickBooks Online?

Managing business finances can be one of the most daunting tasks for small business owners. From tracking expenses and sending invoices to reconciling accounts and generating financial reports, it's easy to feel overwhelmed. That's where **QuickBooks Online** comes in—a robust, cloud-based accounting software designed to simplify and automate your financial processes, saving you time and reducing stress.

1. Accessible Anytime, Anywhere

One of the standout features of QuickBooks Online is its cloud-based functionality. Unlike traditional desktop software, QuickBooks Online allows you to access your financial data from anywhere, whether you're at your office, at home, or on the go. This flexibility is particularly beneficial for small business owners who wear many hats and need to stay connected to their finances even while multitasking.

Imagine you're running errands for your boutique and a customer calls about an invoice. With QuickBooks Online, you can log in from your smartphone, review the invoice, and even send it while you're away from your desk. This convenience ensures you're never disconnected from your business.

2. User-Friendly Interface

QuickBooks Online is designed with ease of use in mind. Its clean, intuitive interface makes it accessible even for those with no prior accounting experience. Navigating through features like invoicing, expense tracking, and financial reporting is straightforward, with helpful prompts guiding you every step of the way.

For someone like you, who may be transitioning from outsourcing bookkeeping to managing it yourself, this simplicity can make a world of difference. QuickBooks Online ensures you spend less time figuring out the software and more time using it to grow your business.

3. Automation for Efficiency

QuickBooks Online excels in automation, which is a game-changer for busy entrepreneurs. Tasks like recurring invoices, bill payments, and transaction categorization can all be automated, freeing up your time for more strategic activities.

For instance, if you have a subscription service as part of your boutique, you can set up recurring invoices that are sent automatically each month. Similarly, QuickBooks can categorize your transactions based on rules you create, saving you from manually sorting through expenses. Automation not only saves time but also minimizes the risk of errors, ensuring your financial records remain accurate and up to date.

4. Tailored for Small Businesses

QuickBooks Online isn't just accounting software—it's a tool specifically designed to address the needs of small business owners. It offers customizable features that adapt to your business model, whether you're a retailer, freelancer, or service provider.

For example, if you run a retail boutique, QuickBooks can help you track inventory levels, monitor cost of goods sold, and set low-stock alerts. These features are vital for ensuring you have the right products available without overstocking and tying up cash flow. Additionally, QuickBooks integrates seamlessly with platforms like Shopify, Square, and PayPal, making it an excellent choice for businesses with e-commerce operations.

5. Comprehensive Reporting and Insights

Financial reports are essential for understanding the health of your business and making informed decisions. QuickBooks Online simplifies this by generating detailed reports like Profit and Loss, Balance Sheet, and Cash Flow statements with just a few clicks.

Even if you're not a financial expert, these reports are presented in an easy-to-understand format, helping you identify trends, spot potential issues, and plan for the future. For instance, reviewing your cash flow report could highlight seasonal patterns in your boutique, allowing you to plan inventory and promotions accordingly.

6. Scalable for Growth

As your business grows, your financial needs will evolve. QuickBooks Online is built to scale with you, offering advanced features like payroll management, budgeting, and multi-user access.

For example, if you hire employees or contractors for your boutique, QuickBooks can handle payroll calculations, tax filings, and direct deposits seamlessly. You can also add team members to your account, assigning specific permissions to ensure your data remains secure. These scalable features mean you won't need to switch software as your business expands.

7. Cloud Security and Regular Updates

QuickBooks Online prioritizes the security of your financial data. It uses bank-level encryption and regularly backs up your data, ensuring it's safe from cyber threats or accidental loss.

Additionally, as a cloud-based tool, QuickBooks Online is continually updated with new features and improvements. You won't need to worry about purchasing or installing updates manually—everything happens automatically, keeping your software current and efficient.

8. Affordable and Flexible Plans

For small businesses, every dollar counts. QuickBooks Online offers several pricing tiers, allowing you to choose a plan that fits your budget and requirements. Whether you're just starting or managing a growing enterprise, there's an option for you.

With a free trial available, you can explore the software before committing, ensuring it's the right fit for your needs. Plus, the potential time and cost savings from automation and improved financial management make QuickBooks Online a worthwhile investment.

9. Community and Support

QuickBooks Online has a vast user community and extensive support resources. From video tutorials and help articles to live customer support, you'll have access to everything you need to succeed.

Additionally, the community forums are filled with real-world advice from other small business owners, providing a valuable network of peers who understand your challenges.

QuickBooks Online is more than just a bookkeeping tool—it's a powerful ally for small business owners. By simplifying financial management, automating repetitive tasks, and providing actionable insights, it helps you focus on what you do best: growing your business.

Whether you're a total beginner or looking to refine your skills, QuickBooks Online offers everything you need to take control of your finances with confidence. This book will guide you step by-step, ensuring you unlock its full potential and transform how you manage your business. Let's get started!

How This 3-in-1 Bundle Is Designed for Your Success

Welcome to the ultimate QuickBooks Online learning experience! This 3-in-1 bundle is more than just a guide—it's a comprehensive roadmap designed to take you from a complete beginner to a confident QuickBooks Online user with advanced, profession-al-level skills. Whether you're a small business owner, freelancer, or just someone eager to manage finances more effectively, this book is crafted with your success in mind.

Let's explore how each part of this bundle is carefully structured to ensure your journey with QuickBooks Online is smooth, prac-tical, and impactful.

1. A Gradual Learning Curve for Confidence and Clarity

Starting with the basics and advancing through intermediate and professional-level features, this bundle is designed to help you build your knowledge step by step. We understand that jumping straight into advanced features can feel overwhelming, especially if you're new to bookkeeping or software like QuickBooks Online. That's why this book is broken down into three distinct sections, or "books," each focusing on a specific level of expertise.

- **Book 1: QuickBooks Online Basics**

This section is your foundation. It introduces you to the core functions of QuickBooks Online, such as setting up your account, customizing your dashboard, and navigating the interface. By the end of this book, you'll be able to perform essential tasks like creating invoices, tracking expenses, and reconciling accounts with confidence.

- **Book 2: Intermediate Tools and Features**

Once you're comfortable with the basics, the second section

deepens your understanding by exploring intermediate features like customer management, app integrations, and automated workflows. This book is all about enhancing your efficiency and tailoring QuickBooks to meet the specific needs of your business.

- **Book 3: Advanced Features and Troubleshooting**

For those ready to go pro, the third book dives into advanced topics such as payroll management, inventory tracking, and custom reporting. You'll also learn troubleshooting techniques and efficiency hacks to master the software and handle any challenges that come your way.

Each section builds upon the previous one, ensuring you're never overwhelmed but always challenged to grow your skills.

2. Actionable Steps and Hands-On Learning

Theory is important, but practical application is where true learning happens. This bundle emphasizes actionable steps, with every chapter offering clear, step-by-step instructions to help you apply what you've learned immediately.

For example, instead of simply explaining how to create an invoice, we'll walk you through the process with detailed guidance, including screenshots, diagrams, and tips. By the time you finish the chapter, you'll not only understand the concept but also have firsthand experience implementing it in your own QuickBooks Online account.

To make the content even more accessible:

- Key processes are broken down into manageable tasks.
- Sections include "Do This Now" prompts to encourage immediate application.
- Summaries and checklists at the end of chapters reinforce learning.

3. Designed for Real-Life Scenarios

As a small business owner or professional, you don't just need abstract explanations—you need solutions tailored to your day-to-day challenges. This book is built with real-world scenarios in mind, offering practical advice that resonates with your business needs.

Imagine you're managing inventory for your boutique, juggling supplier payments, and tracking sales through multiple platforms like Shopify or PayPal. Throughout this book, you'll find examples and workflows that align with these specific situations, making it easier to see how QuickBooks Online fits into your existing processes.

By addressing common pain points—like reconciling accounts, automating repetitive tasks, and generating meaningful financial reports—we ensure you're prepared to handle the realities of running a business.

4. Customizable Tools for Diverse Needs

Every business is unique, and so are its financial management needs. This 3-in-1 bundle acknowledges that by providing guidance on how to customize QuickBooks Online for your specific situation. Whether you're managing a retail boutique, providing freelance services, or running an e-commerce store, this book shows you how to adapt QuickBooks to work for you.

From setting up industry-specific features to tailoring reports and workflows, you'll learn how to make QuickBooks Online your own. This flexibility ensures that the skills you gain are relevant and immediately applicable to your business.

5. Troubleshooting and Pro Tips for Long-Term Success

Software can sometimes feel frustrating, especially when things don't go as planned. This bundle doesn't just teach you how to use QuickBooks Online—it prepares you to troubleshoot common issues and overcome challenges with ease.

In Book 3, we dedicate entire sections to resolving frequent errors, like syncing issues, duplicate transactions, or payroll glitches. Additionally, you'll discover efficiency hacks, keyboard shortcuts, and best practices that save time and simplify your workflow. By mastering these skills, you'll gain the confidence to handle any situation, ensuring your success isn't short-lived but long-term.

6. Supplemental Bonuses for Extra Value

To complement the content in this bundle, we've included two practical bonuses:

- **QuickBooks Online Setup and Efficiency Toolkit**: A guide to setting up your account with ease, including checklists, templates, and time-saving tips.
- **Monthly Accounting and Reporting Planner**: A planner designed to help you stay organized, track tasks, and generate reports efficiently.

These resources are designed to reinforce your learning, making it easier to implement and maintain the skills you've gained.

7. A Focus on Empowerment and Growth

At its core, this bundle is about more than just learning software—it's about empowering you to take control of your finances and grow your business confidently. By mastering QuickBooks Online, you're not only improving your financial management skills but also setting the foundation for smarter decision-making, greater profitability, and sustainable success.

With this 3-in-1 bundle, you're not just learning QuickBooks Online—you're gaining a valuable skill set that will transform the way you manage your business. Whether you're just starting out or ready to unlock advanced features, this book is your trusted companion every step of the way. Let's dive in and start your journey to financial clarity and efficiency!

Who This Book Is For: Beginner to Pro

Every journey begins with a first step, and when it comes to mastering QuickBooks Online, this book is designed to guide you from the very first click to becoming a confident, self-reliant user. Whether you're a complete beginner just starting to explore accounting software or someone with some experience looking to advance your skills, this book caters to all levels. Let's explore who this book is for and how it meets the needs of its diverse audience.

1. The Absolute Beginner

If you've never opened QuickBooks Online before, you might feel overwhelmed by the sheer number of features, options, and settings. This book was created with you in mind, starting with the very basics of setting up your account and understanding the software's interface. We know that accounting jargon and unfamiliar workflows can be intimidating, so we break everything down into simple, digestible steps.

In **Book 1: QuickBooks Online Basics**, we'll walk you through the essential tasks that form the foundation of financial management. You'll learn how to:

- Set up your QuickBooks Online account for the first time.
- Customize the dashboard to fit your workflow.
- Create professional invoices and track expenses effectively.
- Reconcile accounts and generate basic reports.

This section assumes no prior knowledge and focuses on building your confidence. By the end of Book 1, you'll be comfortable navigating QuickBooks Online and handling everyday financial tasks with ease.

2. The Small Business Owner

As a small business owner, you wear many hats—manager, marketer, salesperson, and sometimes even bookkeeper. You don't have time to waste on overly complex systems or irrelevant features. You need actionable advice that addresses the unique challenges of running a small business.

This book is tailored for entrepreneurs like you, whether you're managing a boutique, running a service-based business, or operating an e-commerce store. Throughout the book, you'll find practical examples that resonate with your day-to-day responsibilities, such as:

- Managing inventory and setting low-stock alerts for retail businesses.
- Tracking project expenses and client invoices for service providers.
- Integrating QuickBooks Online with platforms like Shopify, PayPal, or Square for seamless e-commerce operations.

In **Book 2: Intermediate Tools and Features**, you'll learn how to:

- Automate repetitive tasks like recurring invoices and bill payments.
- Use app integrations to streamline workflows and save time.
- Generate insightful reports to understand your business's financial health.

Whether you're just starting out or looking to streamline your processes, this book provides tools and techniques to make your financial management more efficient and less stressful.

3. The Freelancer or Sole Proprietor

Freelancers and sole proprietors often face unique challenges when it comes to managing finances. Without a team or dedicated accountant, you're left to juggle everything on your own. This book simplifies the process, empowering you to handle your bookkeeping with confidence.

QuickBooks Online is an excellent solution for individuals who:

- Want to track income and expenses for tax reporting.
- Need to create and send professional invoices to clients.
- Manage irregular cash flow effectively.

Throughout the book, we offer tips tailored to freelancers, such as categorizing expenses to maximize deductions and setting up custom reports to track project profitability. By the time you finish, you'll have a clear understanding of your financial situation, enabling you to focus on delivering great work to your clients.

4. The Experienced User Looking to Level Up

Maybe you've been using QuickBooks Online for a while but feel like you're only scratching the surface. If you're ready to explore the software's more advanced features and take your financial management skills to the next level, this book will show you how.

In **Book 3: Advanced Features and Troubleshooting**, we dive into professional-level tools and techniques, such as:

- Setting up payroll and managing employee accounts.
- Tracking inventory and understanding the cost of goods sold (COGS).
- Customizing reports and leveraging data for strategic decision-making.

- Troubleshooting common issues like duplicate transactions or syncing errors.

This section is designed for users who want to maximize the value of QuickBooks Online by mastering its full range of capabilities. With advanced skills, you'll not only streamline your bookkeeping but also gain deeper insights into your business's performance.

5. The Time-Strapped Learner

Time is a precious resource, and not everyone has hours to dedicate to learning new software. If you're someone who needs quick, actionable guidance, this book is perfect for you.

Each chapter is structured to be concise and focused, with step-by-step instructions that are easy to follow. Key features include:

- "Do This Now" sections for immediate implementation.
- Tips and tricks to save time, such as keyboard shortcuts and automation tools.
- Summaries and checklists to reinforce learning and track progress.

By breaking down complex processes into manageable steps, this book ensures you can learn efficiently and effectively, even if you're short on time.

6. The Growth-Oriented Business Owner

If you're looking to scale your business, understanding your finances is crucial. QuickBooks Online is a powerful tool for tracking growth, identifying opportunities, and preparing for the future. This book helps you leverage QuickBooks Online to:

- Create budgets and track progress toward financial goals.
- Use advanced reporting to forecast revenue and expenses.
- Prepare for audits or investor presentations with professional, accurate data.

By equipping you with these skills, this book positions you to make smarter financial decisions and drive your business forward.

Who This Book Isn't For

While this book is comprehensive, it's not aimed at experienced accountants or CPAs looking for advanced, technical accounting strategies. Instead, it focuses on empowering non-experts—business owners, freelancers, and new users—to effectively manage their finances using QuickBooks Online.

Whether you're a beginner learning the basics, an intermediate user looking to streamline processes, or an advanced user eager to unlock professional features, this book meets you where you are and guides you toward your goals. With practical examples, actionable advice, and a step-by-step approach, you'll gain the skills and confidence to master QuickBooks Online and take control of your financial future.

This is your guide from beginner to pro, tailored for your unique journey. Let's get started!

A Roadmap to Mastery: What You'll Learn in Each Book

Mastering QuickBooks Online doesn't happen overnight, but with the right guidance and structure, you'll progress smoothly from beginner to pro. This 3-in-1 bundle is designed as a comprehensive roadmap, with each book building on the previous one to ensure you gain confidence, skills, and advanced knowledge step by step. Whether you're setting up QuickBooks Online for the first time or diving into its most powerful features, this roadmap is your guide to success.

Book 1: QuickBooks Online Basics
Foundation for Beginners

The first book in this bundle lays the groundwork by introducing you to the core functions of QuickBooks Online. It's perfect for absolute beginners or anyone who needs a refresher on the basics of financial management. This section assumes no prior experience and focuses on the essential tools and tasks you'll use daily.

Here's what you'll learn in **Book 1**:

- **Getting Started with QuickBooks Online**: Learn how to set up your account, choose the right subscription plan, and configure essential settings for your business.
- **Personalizing QuickBooks for Your Business**: Customize

your dashboard, set up notifications, and tailor features to suit your industry or workflow.

- **Mastering Everyday Features**: Discover how to create and send professional invoices, categorize and track expenses, and connect your bank accounts for seamless transaction imports.
- **Organizing Monthly Finances**: Follow a monthly checklist for reconciling accounts, generating basic reports, and closing the books to prepare for tax season.

By the end of Book 1, you'll feel comfortable navigating Quick-Books Online, performing day-to-day tasks, and understanding how the software can simplify your financial management.

Book 2: Intermediate Tools and Features

Building Efficiency and Control

Once you've mastered the basics, it's time to expand your knowledge with the intermediate features of QuickBooks Online. Book 2 focuses on efficiency, automation, and customization, helping you save time and gain more control over your finances.

Here's what you'll learn in **Book 2**:

- **Mastering the Navigation Bar**: Learn how to make the most of the interface, customize shortcuts, and use the interactive dashboard to monitor your business's performance.
- **Sales and Customer Management**: Create estimates, send recurring invoices, track customer payments, and handle refunds with ease.
- **Streamlining Expense Management**: Set up vendor profiles, automate recurring bill payments, and use mileage tracking tools to log expenses accurately.
- **Boosting Productivity with App Integrations**: Connect QuickBooks Online to popular apps like Shopify, PayPal, and Square. Learn how to sync inventory tools, improve transaction management, and troubleshoot common integration issues.

By the end of Book 2, you'll be managing your finances more efficiently, freeing up time for other aspects of your business, and customizing QuickBooks Online to meet your unique needs.

Book 3: Advanced Features and Troubleshooting

Going Pro with Advanced Tools

The final book in this bundle is all about unlocking the full potential of QuickBooks Online. Designed for experienced users or those who want to explore the software's most powerful features, Book 3 takes your financial management skills to the professional level.

Here's what you'll learn in **Book 3**:

- **Payroll and Employee Management**: Set up payroll, automate tax calculations, and manage employee payments. Learn how to use self-service portals for employees to access their pay stubs and W-2s.
- **Inventory and Budgeting**: Track inventory levels, manage the cost of goods sold (COGS), and create budgets to align with your financial goals. Discover how to use low-stock alerts and reorder points to maintain smooth operations.
- **Advanced Reporting and Analytics**: Customize reports for specific business needs, use forecasting tools to predict growth, and analyze data to make informed decisions. Explore audit logs to maintain data integrity and track changes.
- **Troubleshooting and Efficiency Hacks**: Handle common errors like duplicate transactions, syncing issues, and login problems. Learn time-saving tricks, including keyboard shortcuts, custom fields, and best practices for organized bookkeeping.

By the end of Book 3, you'll be a QuickBooks Online expert, capable of tackling complex tasks, troubleshooting problems, and using advanced features to optimize your business's financial management.

How the Books Work Together

This 3-in-1 bundle is designed to create a seamless learning experience. Each book builds on the skills learned in the previous one, allowing you to progress naturally from beginner to advanced user. Here's how the structure ensures your mastery of QuickBooks Online:

1. **Learn the Basics**: Start with essential tasks to establish a strong foundation.
2. **Expand Your Skills**: Delve into intermediate features that enhance efficiency and productivity.
3. **Go Pro**: Explore advanced tools and techniques for complete financial control.

Whether you choose to read all three books sequentially or skip ahead to specific sections that meet your current needs, this bundle offers flexibility while ensuring comprehensive coverage.

Why This Roadmap Works

1. **Step-by-Step Progression**: You'll never feel overwhelmed because each chapter builds on the previous one, reinforcing your learning.
2. **Actionable Guidance**: Clear instructions and real-world examples make it easy to apply what you've learned immediately.
3. **Comprehensive Coverage**: From basics to advanced tools, every aspect of QuickBooks Online is covered.

This roadmap is more than a guide—it's your partner in mastering QuickBooks Online. By the time you finish this bundle, you'll not only understand the software but also feel empowered to use it effectively, saving time, reducing stress, and making smarter financial decisions.

Are you ready to begin your journey from beginner to pro? Let's get started!

BOOK 1

QUICKBOOKS ONLINE BASICS

Welcome to **Book 1: QuickBooks Online Basics**, the essential starting point for anyone new to QuickBooks Online. Whether you're a small business owner, a freelancer, or someone transitioning to digital bookkeeping, this book is designed to provide you with the foundational knowledge and skills to confidently manage your finances.

QuickBooks Online is a powerful tool for streamlining your accounting, but its many features can feel overwhelming for beginners. That's why this book starts at the very beginning, breaking down the fundamentals into clear, actionable steps. From setting up your account to navigating the interface and completing daily tasks, you'll gain the confidence to use QuickBooks Online efficiently and effectively.

This book focuses on real-world scenarios to help you understand how QuickBooks Online fits into your unique business needs. You'll learn how to personalize the dashboard for your workflow, create invoices, track expenses, and generate reports that give you a clear picture of your financial health.

By the end of **Book 1**, you'll have a solid foundation, enabling you to handle everyday financial management tasks with ease. With this knowledge, you'll be ready to move forward and explore the more advanced tools and features covered in later books. Let's get started!

CHAPTER 1
GETTING STARTED WITH QUICKBOOKS ONLINE

Getting started with QuickBooks Online is an exciting first step toward simplifying and mastering your business finances. As a small business owner, managing your financial data can feel overwhelming, but QuickBooks Online offers an intuitive, efficient solution to take the stress out of bookkeeping.

In this chapter, we'll introduce you to the key benefits of using QuickBooks Online and why it's the go-to accounting software for millions of small business owners worldwide. You'll discover how it streamlines essential tasks like invoicing, expense tracking, and financial reporting, saving you time and helping you stay organized. Whether you're managing your business solo or collaborating with a team, QuickBooks Online provides the tools you need to maintain clarity and control over your finances.

We'll guide you through the step-by-step process of setting up your QuickBooks Online account, ensuring you choose the right subscription plan and configure your settings to align with your business needs. Finally, you'll learn how to navigate QuickBooks Online across multiple devices, from your desktop to your smartphone, giving you the flexibility to manage your finances anytime, anywhere.

By the end of this chapter, you'll have a fully functional QuickBooks Online account and the confidence to begin exploring its core features. Let's dive in and take the first steps toward financial efficiency!

Understanding QuickBooks Online: Benefits for Small Business Owners

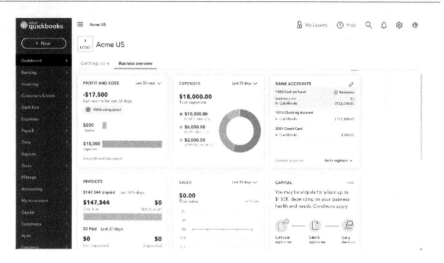

Managing finances is one of the most critical aspects of running a successful business, yet it's also one of the most challenging. As a small business owner, you often wear multiple hats, juggling everything from sales and marketing to operations and customer service. Adding financial management to this mix can feel overwhelming, especially if you're not an accounting expert. That's where **QuickBooks Online** comes in—a comprehensive and user-friendly tool designed to simplify your bookkeeping and put you in control of your finances.

In this section, we'll explore the many benefits of QuickBooks Online for small business owners, highlighting how it can save you time, improve accuracy, and provide valuable insights to help your business thrive.

1. Simplifying Financial Management

One of the biggest advantages of QuickBooks Online is its ability to centralize and streamline your financial management tasks. Instead of juggling spreadsheets, receipts, and separate software for invoicing and expense tracking, QuickBooks brings everything together in one platform.

With QuickBooks Online, you can:

- **Track income and expenses**: Easily categorize transactions to see exactly where your money is going.
- **Create professional invoices**: Send customized invoices directly to clients and track their payment status.
- **Monitor cash flow**: Access real-time data to keep tabs on your income and expenses.
- **Reconcile accounts**: Match your bank transactions with your financial records to ensure accuracy.

By having all your financial data in one place, QuickBooks Online reduces the risk of errors, eliminates duplicate efforts, and gives you a clear overview of your business's financial health.

2. Accessible Anytime, Anywhere

As a cloud-based platform, QuickBooks Online offers unmatched flexibility. Whether you're working from your office, meeting with clients, or on the go, you can access your financial data from any device with an internet connection. This is especially beneficial for small business owners who need to stay connected to their finances at all times.

For instance:

- You can check your cash flow while waiting for a client meeting.
- You can send an invoice directly from your phone after completing a project.
- Your accountant or bookkeeper can access your records remotely, eliminating the need for in-person visits or sharing files manually.

This accessibility ensures you're always in control, no matter where you are, and allows you to make informed decisions in real-time.

3. User-Friendly Interface

QuickBooks Online is designed with small business owners in mind, offering an intuitive and easy-to-navigate interface. Even if you have no prior experience with accounting software, you'll find it straightforward to use.

The dashboard provides a clear snapshot of your financial data, including:

- **Income and expenses**: A real-time summary of your financial position.
- **Invoices and payments**: An overview of outstanding invoices and recently received payments.
- **Profit and loss**: Quick access to your key financial metrics.

Additionally, QuickBooks Online offers guided tutorials, prompts, and a robust help center to assist you as you explore its features. This ease of use allows you to focus on running your business rather than worrying about technical difficulties.

4. Automation for Efficiency

Time is one of the most valuable resources for small business owners, and QuickBooks Online excels in automating repetitive tasks to help you save more of it.

Key automation features include:

- **Recurring invoices**: Set up invoices to send automatically at regular intervals, perfect for subscription-based businesses or ongoing projects.
- **Transaction categorization**: QuickBooks learns how you categorize transactions and applies rules automatically to save time.
- **Bank feeds**: Connect your bank account to automatically import and categorize transactions.
- **Bill payments**: Schedule and automate bill payments to avoid late fees.

Automation not only speeds up your workflows but also reduces the likelihood of errors, ensuring your records remain accurate and up to date.

5. Customization to Suit Your Business

Every business is unique, and QuickBooks Online understands that. Its customizable features allow you to tailor the platform to meet your specific needs.

For example:

- **Industry-specific settings**: QuickBooks offers specialized features for industries like retail, construction, and professional services.

- **Customizable invoices**: Add your logo, adjust the layout, and include personalized messages for a professional touch.
- **Reports and dashboards**: Generate custom reports to track the metrics that matter most to your business.

This flexibility ensures that QuickBooks Online adapts to your business rather than forcing you to conform to a rigid system.

6. Valuable Insights with Reports

Understanding your business's financial health is crucial for making informed decisions, and QuickBooks Online makes this easier with its reporting features.

Some of the key reports you can generate include:

- **Profit and Loss (P&L)**: See your income, expenses, and net profit over a specific period.
- **Balance Sheet**: View your assets, liabilities, and equity at a glance.
- **Cash Flow Statement**: Track the movement of money in and out of your business.
- **A/R and A/P Reports**: Monitor outstanding invoices and bills to stay on top of your accounts receivable and payable.

These reports are not only easy to generate but also simple to interpret, even if you're not a financial expert. They provide actionable insights that help you identify trends, manage cash flow, and plan for the future.

7. Scalability for Growth

As your business grows, your financial needs will evolve. QuickBooks Online is built to scale with you, offering advanced features and integrations that support your growth.

Some examples of scalable features include:

- **Payroll management**: Add payroll services to handle employee wages, taxes, and benefits.
- **Inventory tracking**: Manage stock levels, monitor costs, and set reorder points.
- **Multi-user access**: Collaborate with team members or accountants while maintaining control over permissions.

By investing in QuickBooks Online, you're not just choosing a tool for today—you're selecting a platform that will grow alongside your business.

8. Integration with Other Tools

QuickBooks Online integrates seamlessly with a wide range of apps and tools, allowing you to create a connected ecosystem for your business.

Popular integrations include:

- **E-commerce platforms**: Shopify, WooCommerce, and Big-Commerce.
- **Payment processors**: PayPal, Square, and Stripe.
- **CRM tools**: HubSpot and Salesforce.

These integrations enhance QuickBooks Online's functionality, streamlining processes like payment collection, inventory management, and customer relationship management.

9. Enhanced Security and Support

QuickBooks Online prioritizes the security of your financial data with features like:

- **Bank-level encryption**: Protecting your information from unauthorized access.
- **Regular backups**: Ensuring your data is safe even in the event of a system failure.
- **Two-factor authentication**: Adding an extra layer of protection for your account.

In addition, QuickBooks Online offers extensive support resources, including live chat, phone support, and a community forum where you can connect with other users.

10. Cost-Effective for Small Businesses

Finally, QuickBooks Online offers affordable pricing plans to fit a variety of budgets. Whether you're a sole proprietor or a growing business with multiple employees, there's a plan that meets your needs without breaking the bank.

By streamlining your financial management and providing valuable insights, QuickBooks Online delivers excellent value for money, making it a smart investment for your business.

QuickBooks Online is more than just an accounting tool—it's a comprehensive solution designed to simplify your financial management, save you time, and provide insights that help your business thrive. Whether you're just starting out or looking for ways to improve efficiency, QuickBooks Online offers the features and flexibility to meet your needs. With its user-friendly interface, automation capabilities, and robust reporting tools, it empowers small business owners to take control of their finances and focus on what they do best: growing their business.

Let's continue this journey by diving into the setup process and exploring how to make QuickBooks Online work for your unique needs.

Setting Up Your Account: Step-by-Step Setup and Selecting the Right Plan

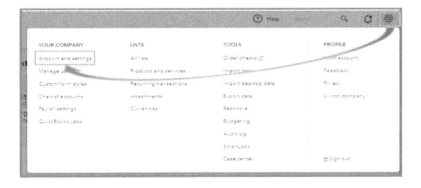

Setting up your QuickBooks Online account is the first and most important step to harnessing the power of this accounting software. This chapter will walk you through the process of creating an account, choosing the plan that best fits your needs, and configuring essential settings. Whether you're new to QuickBooks or transitioning from another platform, following these steps will ensure a smooth start to managing your finances effectively.

Step 1: Choosing the Right QuickBooks Online Plan

QuickBooks Online offers several subscription plans, each designed to meet the needs of different types of businesses. Selecting the right plan is crucial to ensure you're not overpaying for features you don't need or missing out on tools essential to your operations.

Plan Options:

1. Simple Start:

- Ideal for freelancers or sole proprietors.
- Features: Invoicing, expense tracking, basic reporting, and tax deduction tools.

2. Essentials:

- Perfect for small businesses with a few employees or contractors.
- Features: All Simple Start features, plus bill management and multi-user access.

3. Plus:

- Best for growing businesses with inventory or project tracking needs.
- Features: All Essentials features, plus inventory management and budgeting tools.

4. Advanced:

- Designed for larger businesses needing advanced reporting and analytics.
- Features: All Plus features, plus custom reports, dedicated account support, and workflow automation.

How to Choose:

- **Evaluate your business size and complexity.** Freelancers and sole proprietors may find Simple Start sufficient, while retailers with inventory or businesses managing multiple users will benefit from the Plus plan.
- **Consider future needs.** If you plan to scale, selecting a plan with advanced features like inventory tracking or custom reporting can save you from switching later.
- **Budget wisely.** Start with a plan that meets your current needs. You can always upgrade as your business grows.

Step 2: Creating Your QuickBooks Online Account

Once you've chosen your plan, it's time to create your account. QuickBooks Online's setup process is user-friendly, guiding you through the initial configuration step by step.

1. **Visit the QuickBooks Online Website:**

Go to QuickBooks Online and click on "Sign Up" or "Free Trial" to begin.

2. **Select Your Plan:**

Choose the subscription plan that aligns with your business needs. QuickBooks often offers free trials, allowing you to explore features before committing.

3. **Create an Account:**

- Enter your email address, create a password, and provide your contact details.
- Confirm your email address through the verification link sent to your inbox.

4. **Provide Business Details:**

- Enter your business name, industry, and the type of business entity (e.g., sole proprietor, partnership, LLC).
- Select your time zone and country to ensure proper date formatting and tax calculations.

5. **Set Up Your Business Logo (Optional):**

Upload your logo to personalize your invoices and reports. While optional, it enhances your brand's professional appearance.

Step 3: Configuring Basic Settings

With your account created, the next step is configuring Quick-Books Online to align with your business operations. Proper configuration ensures your account is tailored to your needs and eliminates potential headaches down the line.

1. **Set Up Your Chart of Accounts:**

The Chart of Accounts is a list of all the categories used to track your business's income, expenses, assets, and liabilities. Quick-Books provides a default chart based on your industry, but you can customize it to fit your business.

- Add categories specific to your operations (e.g., "Supplies" for a boutique or "Software Subscriptions" for a freelancer).
- Delete unused categories to keep things organized.

2. Customize Invoice Templates:

- Navigate to the "Invoicing" section and select "Customize Invoice."
- Add your logo, adjust the layout, and include custom fields like payment terms or notes.

3. Connect Your Bank Accounts:

- Link your business checking and credit card accounts to automate transaction imports.
- QuickBooks will sync with your bank, categorizing transactions for review and approval.

4. Set Up Sales Tax:

- If you charge sales tax, enable this feature in the "Taxes" menu.
- Enter your tax rates, jurisdictions, and any exemptions specific to your business.

5. Add Users and Set Permissions (if applicable):

- For multi-user plans like Essentials or Plus, invite team members and assign roles.
- Grant permissions based on job functions, such as limiting access to sensitive data for certain users.

Step 4: Importing Data

If you're transitioning from another platform or have existing financial data, importing this information into QuickBooks Online will save time and maintain continuity.

1. Gather Your Financial Records:

- Export data from your previous accounting software in CSV format.
- Include key information like customer and vendor lists, product inventories, and previous transactions.

2. Import into QuickBooks Online:

- Go to the "Settings" menu and select "Import Data."
- Upload CSV files for each category (customers, vendors, prod-

ucts, etc.). QuickBooks provides templates to ensure com-patibility.

3. **Verify Imported Data:**

Review your data after importing to ensure accuracy. Correct any discrepancies before moving forward.

Step 5: Exploring the Dashboard

QuickBooks Online's dashboard is your central hub, providing a real-time overview of your business's financial health. Spend time familiarizing yourself with its key components:

1. **Navigation Menu:**

Located on the left, this menu provides access to essential features like Sales, Expenses, Reports, and Banking.

2. **Dashboard Widgets:**

- **Cash Flow:** See a snapshot of your income, expenses, and cash flow trends.
- **Invoices and Payments:** View overdue invoices and recently received payments.
- **Expenses:** Monitor spending and categorize transactions.

3. **Search Bar:**

Quickly locate transactions, customers, or vendors using this tool.

Step 6: Testing and Finalizing Setup

Before diving into daily use, test your QuickBooks Online account to ensure everything is functioning as expected.

1. **Create a Test Invoice:** Send a test invoice to yourself to confirm that the template, payment methods, and email delivery are set up correctly.
2. **Record a Test Expense:** Enter a small expense to familiarize yourself with transaction categorization.
3. **Run a Basic Report:** Generate a Profit and Loss report to ensure your data is being tracked and displayed accurately.
4. **Review Account Settings:** Double-check your settings for accuracy, including tax rates, permissions, and payment preferences.

Step 7: Tips for a Smooth Transition

If you're new to accounting software or switching from another platform, keep these tips in mind to make the transition as smooth as possible:

- **Start Fresh:** Avoid importing unnecessary data to keep your QuickBooks Online account organized.
- **Take Your Time:** Explore features gradually instead of trying to master everything at once.
- **Seek Support:** Use QuickBooks Online's Help Center or contact customer support if you encounter issues.

Setting up your QuickBooks Online account is a straightforward but vital process that sets the foundation for effective financial management. By selecting the right plan, configuring your account, and familiarizing yourself with the dashboard, you'll be well-prepared to handle your business's finances efficiently. Once your account is ready, you can begin leveraging QuickBooks Online's powerful features to streamline your operations, save time, and gain valuable insights into your business's performance. Let's move forward and explore how to navigate QuickBooks Online with confidence.

Navigating Accessibility: Using QuickBooks Across Devices Securely

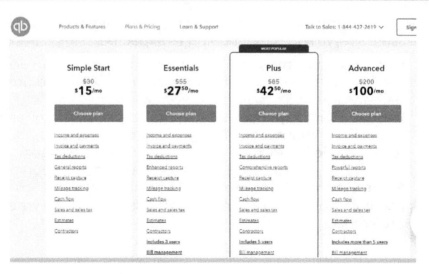

One of the greatest strengths of QuickBooks Online is its cloud-based nature, allowing you to access your financial data anytime, anywhere, and from virtually any device. Whether you're working from your desktop computer, reviewing financial reports on your tablet, or sending invoices from your smartphone, QuickBooks Online makes it easy to stay connected to your business's finances.

However, with this convenience comes the need for secure usage to protect sensitive financial information. In this section, we'll explore how to effectively navigate QuickBooks Online across multiple devices while ensuring security and efficiency.

1. The Power of Cloud-Based Access

QuickBooks Online leverages cloud technology, giving you the ability to manage your finances from any device with an internet connection. This accessibility eliminates the need for traditional desktop software, offering unparalleled flexibility for busy business owners.

Benefits of Cloud Access:

- **Remote Work Capability:** Access QuickBooks Online from your office, home, or on the go.
- **Real-Time Updates:** Any changes made on one device are instantly reflected across all devices.
- **Multi-User Collaboration:** Team members or accountants can log in remotely to assist with bookkeeping or audits.

For example, imagine you're traveling for a business conference, and a client calls with a question about their invoice. Instead of waiting to return to your office, you can pull up the invoice on your phone, provide immediate answers, and even send a payment reminder—all while on the move.

2. Accessing QuickBooks Online Across Devices

QuickBooks Online on Desktop:

For in-depth financial management tasks, a desktop or laptop provides the most robust experience.

- Use a web browser like Chrome, Firefox, or Edge to log in to QuickBooks Online.
- Features such as detailed reporting, batch transactions, and advanced customizations are best suited for desktop usage.

- Desktop access is ideal for tasks that require multiple screens or extensive data entry, such as reconciling accounts or generating year-end reports.

QuickBooks Online Mobile App:

The QuickBooks Online mobile app, available on iOS and Android, is perfect for on-the-go access.

- Features include creating and sending invoices, capturing expense receipts, and viewing key financial data.
- The app's intuitive interface is designed for quick, task-oriented actions rather than extensive data analysis.
- Push notifications alert you to overdue invoices, low-stock inventory, or other critical updates.

QuickBooks Online on Tablets:

Tablets offer a middle ground between the mobile app and desktop experience.

- Use the mobile app for tasks requiring portability but with the added benefit of a larger screen.
- Tablets are particularly useful for tasks like reviewing reports, approving transactions, or conducting client presentations.

3. Managing Multi-User Access

QuickBooks Online allows for multiple users to access the same account, making it an excellent tool for collaboration. However, managing these users effectively and securely is critical.

Adding Users:

- Navigate to the "Settings" menu and select "Manage Users."
- Invite users by entering their email addresses and assigning roles (e.g., Accountant, Standard User).

Role-Based Permissions:

QuickBooks Online offers customizable permissions, ensuring users can only access the data they need.

- **Admin:** Full access to all features and data.
- **Standard User:** Limited access based on assigned permissions (e.g., sales only, expenses only).
- **Reports Only:** Access to view and generate reports without editing data.

Best Practices for Multi-User Access:

- Limit administrative privileges to trusted individuals.
- Regularly review user roles and remove access for former employees or contractors.
- Enable activity tracking to monitor changes made by users.

4. Securing Your QuickBooks Online Account

The flexibility of cloud-based access also requires proactive measures to protect sensitive financial information. QuickBooks Online includes several built-in security features, but additional steps can further enhance protection.

Using Strong Passwords:

A strong password is your first line of defense.

- Create passwords with at least 12 characters, using a mix of uppercase letters, lowercase letters, numbers, and symbols.
- Avoid using easily guessable information like your business name or birthdate.

Enabling Two-Factor Authentication (2FA):

QuickBooks Online supports two-factor authentication, adding an extra layer of security to your account.

- When logging in, 2FA requires a code sent to your mobile device or email in addition to your password.
- Enable this feature under the "Security" settings for maximum protection.

Restricting Device Access:

Limit QuickBooks access to trusted devices.

- Avoid logging in on public computers or unsecured networks.
- Use a virtual private network (VPN) for secure access when working on public Wi-Fi.

Monitoring Login Activity:

Regularly review your account's login history to detect unauthorized access.

- Navigate to the "Settings" menu and select "Account Activity."
- Look for unfamiliar devices or login attempts and change your password immediately if suspicious activity is detected.

5. Syncing Across Devices

One of QuickBooks Online's standout features is its ability to sync data seamlessly across all devices. Whether you enter an invoice on your desktop or capture a receipt on your smartphone, the information is updated in real-time.

Key Syncing Features:

- **Bank Transactions:** Automatically imported and categorized from linked accounts.
- **Invoices and Payments:** Updates reflect immediately, showing whether an invoice has been paid or remains overdue.
- **Reports:** Generate updated reports with the most recent data, regardless of which device was used to input the information.

Syncing ensures accuracy and eliminates the risk of duplicate data entry, saving you time and reducing errors.

6. Troubleshooting Device Accessibility

While QuickBooks Online is designed for seamless cross-device use, occasional technical issues can arise. Here's how to troubleshoot common problems:

Issue: Difficulty Logging In

- Ensure you're using the correct login credentials.
- Clear your browser cache or update the QuickBooks app to the latest version.
- Check your internet connection.

Issue: Data Not Syncing

- Confirm that all devices are connected to the internet.
- Log out and log back in to refresh your session.
- Contact QuickBooks Online support if the issue persists.

Issue: Slow Performance on Mobile Devices

- Close other apps running in the background to free up memory.
- Update your device's operating system and the QuickBooks app.

7. Leveraging Accessibility for Growth

The ability to access QuickBooks Online from anywhere allows you to operate your business more efficiently and flexibly. For instance:

- Review cash flow while traveling to ensure you have funds for a purchase.
- Approve a bill or payment request from a team member without returning to your office.
- Quickly access and share financial reports with potential investors or partners during meetings.

By fully utilizing QuickBooks Online's cross-device accessibility, you can make informed decisions faster and stay ahead in a competitive business environment.

8. Balancing Accessibility and Security

While accessibility is a key benefit, maintaining security is non-negotiable. Balancing convenience with safety ensures your financial data remains protected while you enjoy the flexibility of cloud-based access.

Tips for Balancing Accessibility and Security:

- Always log out of QuickBooks Online on shared or public devices.
- Regularly update your passwords and security settings.

- Educate your team on secure login practices and the importance of protecting sensitive data.

QuickBooks Online's cross-device accessibility revolutionizes how small business owners manage their finances. Whether you're at your desk, on your phone, or working from a tablet, the ability to access real-time financial data ensures you're always in control. By leveraging this flexibility while implementing strong security practices, you can confidently use QuickBooks Online to streamline your operations, save time, and make smarter business decisions.

With these tools and insights in hand, you're now ready to navigate QuickBooks Online across devices effectively and securely. Let's explore how to personalize QuickBooks to make it work even better for your business in the next chapter.

CHAPTER 2

PERSONALIZING QUICKBOOKS FOR YOUR BUSINESS

Every business is unique, and your financial management tools should reflect that. QuickBooks Online is designed to be highly customizable, allowing you to tailor its features and interface to suit your specific needs. In this chapter, we'll explore how to personalize QuickBooks Online so that it works seamlessly with your business operations, whether you're a retailer, a service provider, or a freelancer.

We'll begin by diving into the **dashboard customization** options, where you'll learn how to arrange and modify the interface to prioritize the tools and data you use most frequently. A personalized dashboard ensures you can access essential information like cash flow, invoices, and expenses at a glance.

Next, we'll guide you through **industry-specific settings**, showing you how to optimize QuickBooks for your business type. Whether you're managing inventory for a boutique, tracking billable hours for a service business, or categorizing expenses for freelancing, this section will help you align QuickBooks with your unique workflow.

Finally, we'll cover **notifications and permissions**, ensuring you never miss an important deadline or task while maintaining control over who can access sensitive data. Properly configuring these settings keeps your financial management efficient, organized, and secure.

By the end of this chapter, you'll have a fully customized QuickBooks Online account that saves time, reduces errors, and supports your business's specific goals. Let's get started with transforming QuickBooks into a tool that works perfectly for you!

Customizing the Dashboard: Making QuickBooks Work for You

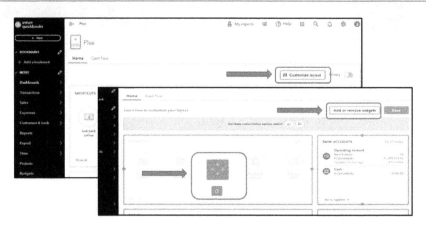

The QuickBooks Online dashboard is your command center, offering a real-time snapshot of your business's financial health. Customizing the dashboard to suit your specific needs can dramatically improve your workflow, helping you focus on the metrics and tools that matter most. Instead of navigating through unnecessary menus or searching for critical data, a personalized dashboard puts everything you need front and center. This chapter will guide you through the process of tailoring the QuickBooks Online dashboard to optimize your financial management.

1. Understanding the Dashboard Components

Before you start customizing, it's important to understand the default elements of the QuickBooks Online dashboard and how they function. The dashboard typically includes:

- **Cash Flow Widget**: A real-time summary of money coming in and going out.
- **Invoices Section**: An overview of outstanding invoices and payments received.
- **Expenses Overview**: A breakdown of recent spending, often categorized by type.

- **Profit and Loss Summary**: A quick look at your revenue, expenses, and net profit.
- **Bank Accounts and Credit Cards**: A list of connected accounts with their current balances.

Each of these elements provides valuable insights, but not all may be relevant to your business. Customizing the dashboard allows you to prioritize the widgets and features that align with your goals.

2. Customizing the Layout

QuickBooks Online gives you the flexibility to arrange the dashboard widgets in a way that suits your workflow. To customize the layout:

1. **Log in to Your Account**: Access your QuickBooks Online account through a web browser.
2. **Navigate to the Dashboard**: The dashboard is the first screen you see upon logging in.
3. **Rearrange Widgets**: Hover over the widget's header, then click and drag it to your desired position.

For example:

- Place the **Cash Flow Widget** at the top if monitoring your cash flow is a daily priority.
- Move the **Profit and Loss Summary** closer to the center if you frequently assess your overall profitability.
- Push less relevant widgets, like bank account balances, to the bottom if they don't require immediate attention.

This drag-and-drop functionality ensures your most critical data is always within easy reach.

3. Choosing Relevant Widgets

While the default widgets are helpful, QuickBooks Online allows you to customize which widgets appear on your dashboard. To add or remove widgets:

1. **Click on the Gear Icon**: Located at the top right corner of the dashboard.
2. **Select "Customize Dashboard"**: This opens a menu with available widgets.

3. **Add or Remove Widgets**: Check or uncheck boxes next to the widgets you want to display or hide.

Examples of Customization:

*   **For Retail Businesses**: Add inventory-related widgets to monitor stock levels and sales trends.
*   **For Service Providers**: Include billable hours or project summaries to keep track of ongoing work.
*   **For Freelancers**: Highlight the invoicing and expenses widgets to manage cash flow and tax deductions.

Customizing widgets ensures that your dashboard reflects the specific needs of your business, streamlining your daily operations.

4. Creating Custom Shortcuts

Another powerful feature of QuickBooks Online is the ability to create shortcuts for frequently used tools. These shortcuts can save you significant time, reducing the need to navigate through multiple menus.

1. **Access the Shortcuts Menu**: Located on the left-hand navigation bar.
2. **Add a Shortcut**: Click the "+ Add Shortcut" button, then select the feature you want to include.
3. **Arrange Shortcuts**: Drag and drop shortcuts into your preferred order.

Common Shortcuts:

*   "Create Invoice" for quick invoicing.
*   "Record Expense" for tracking new purchases.
*   "Generate Report" for fast access to financial summaries.

These shortcuts allow you to perform essential tasks with just a few clicks, enhancing efficiency.

5. Customizing Notifications

Notifications are a vital part of staying on top of your business finances. QuickBooks Online lets you customize notifications to ensure you receive timely reminders for critical tasks without being overwhelmed by unnecessary alerts.

1. **Navigate to Notification Settings**: Click on the Gear Icon, then select "Notifications."

2. **Select Notification Types**: Choose from options like overdue invoices, low-stock inventory, or upcoming bill due dates.
3. **Set Delivery Preferences**: Opt to receive notifications via email, text message, or within the QuickBooks app.

Best Practices:

- Enable notifications for overdue invoices to follow up with clients promptly.
- Turn on reminders for bill payments to avoid late fees.
- Disable less critical notifications to reduce distractions.

Customizing notifications ensures you stay informed about the tasks that matter most without being bogged down by irrelevant updates.

6. Leveraging Custom Reports on the Dashboard

QuickBooks Online allows you to create custom reports and display key data directly on your dashboard. This feature is particularly useful for tracking specific metrics that aren't covered by default widgets.

1. **Create a Custom Report**:

- Go to the "Reports" section in the left-hand menu.
- Select a template (e.g., Profit and Loss, Balance Sheet) and customize filters like date range, account type, or customer name.
- Save the report for future use.

2. **Pin the Report to the Dashboard**:

- Return to the dashboard and select "Customize Dashboard."
- Add the saved report to your list of widgets.

Examples of Custom Reports:

- **Retailers**: A sales summary by product category.
- **Service Providers**: A report tracking hours worked by project.
- **Freelancers**: A detailed breakdown of income sources.

These reports provide actionable insights tailored to your business, making it easier to monitor performance and plan strategically.

7. Mobile Dashboard Customization

If you frequently use the QuickBooks Online mobile app, customizing the dashboard on your smartphone or tablet is equally important. While the app offers fewer customization options than the desktop version, you can still adjust key settings to enhance usability.

1. **Log in to the Mobile App**: Access QuickBooks Online through the iOS or Android app.
2. **Adjust Home Screen Widgets**: Use the "Customize Home" feature to add, remove, or rearrange widgets like invoices, expenses, or cash flow.
3. **Enable Mobile Notifications**: Customize mobile-specific notifications to stay informed while on the go.

A personalized mobile dashboard ensures you can manage your finances efficiently, even when you're away from your desk.

8. Best Practices for Dashboard Customization

To maximize the benefits of your customized dashboard, follow these best practices:

- **Review Periodically**: Reevaluate your dashboard setup every few months to ensure it still aligns with your priorities.
- **Focus on Actionable Data**: Prioritize widgets and reports that inform decisions or highlight tasks requiring immediate attention.
- **Avoid Clutter**: Resist the urge to include too many widgets. A clean, streamlined dashboard improves focus and usability.

Customizing the QuickBooks Online dashboard is one of the simplest yet most effective ways to improve your financial management. By tailoring the layout, widgets, and shortcuts to match your unique business needs, you can save time, reduce errors, and gain instant access to the data that matters most. Whether you're a retailer monitoring inventory, a service provider tracking projects, or a freelancer managing invoices and expenses, a personalized dashboard ensures QuickBooks Online works for you—not the other way around.

Take the time to customize your dashboard today, and enjoy the benefits of a more efficient and organized workflow. With your dashboard set up to support your goals, you'll be ready to dive deeper into the specific features that make QuickBooks Online an indispensable tool for small businesses. Let's move forward to tailoring features by industry in the next section.

Tailoring Features by Industry: Retail, Service-Based, and Freelancer Setups

One of the standout features of QuickBooks Online is its ability to adapt to the specific needs of different industries. Whether you're managing a retail store, running a service-based business, or working as a freelancer, QuickBooks offers tools and customization options that align with your unique workflows. By tailoring the platform to suit your industry, you can streamline operations, save time, and ensure accurate financial management.

This chapter will guide you through industry-specific features and best practices for optimizing QuickBooks Online for **retail businesses**, **service-based businesses**, and **freelancers**.

1. Retail Businesses: Managing Inventory, Sales, and Customers

Retail businesses have distinct financial needs, particularly when it comes to managing inventory and tracking sales. QuickBooks

Online offers robust tools to help retailers stay organized and maintain visibility into their operations.

Key Features for Retail Businesses

1. Inventory Management

- Track inventory levels in real-time to avoid overstocking or running out of popular items.
- Monitor the cost of goods sold (COGS) to understand how inventory affects profitability.
- Set up low-stock alerts to receive notifications when it's time to reorder products.

2. How to Set Up Inventory Management:

- Go to the "Sales" tab and select "Products and Services."
- Add your inventory items, including details like SKU, purchase price, and selling price.
- Enable the inventory tracking feature to automatically adjust stock levels based on sales and purchases.

3. Sales Tracking

- Record sales by product or category to analyze performance.
- Use payment integrations like PayPal, Square, or Shopify to sync sales data automatically.

4. Pro Tip:

Create custom sales reports to identify your best-selling products and peak sales periods, allowing you to optimize your inventory and marketing strategies.

5. Customer Management

- Use the "Customers" tab to create and manage customer profiles.
- Track purchase history to identify repeat customers and create loyalty programs.
- Send personalized invoices and receipts for a professional touch.

6. Tax Tracking

- Enable sales tax tracking to calculate and collect the correct taxes for each transaction.

- Use QuickBooks Online's tax tools to prepare and file sales tax returns easily.

2. Service-Based Businesses: Tracking Projects, Time, and Expenses

Service-based businesses often deal with projects, billable hours, and client-specific expenses. QuickBooks Online provides tools to simplify these processes, ensuring you stay on top of your financial management while delivering exceptional service.

Key Features for Service-Based Businesses

1. **Project Management**

- Use the Projects feature to track income, expenses, and profitability for individual projects.
- Allocate expenses and payments to specific projects for detailed insights.

2. **How to Use Projects in QuickBooks Online:**

- Enable the Projects feature in the "Settings" menu.
- Create a new project and link it to a customer.
- Assign transactions (e.g., expenses, invoices, payments) to the project for accurate tracking.

3. **Pro Tip:**

Generate a Project Profitability Report to identify which projects are the most lucrative.

4. **Time Tracking**

- Log billable hours directly in QuickBooks Online or integrate with time-tracking apps like TSheets.
- Automatically convert logged hours into invoices, ensuring accurate billing.

5. **How to Enable Time Tracking:**

- Navigate to "Settings," then select "Time Tracking."
- Enable the feature and set preferences for billable rates.

6. **Example Use Case:**

A marketing agency can use time tracking to monitor hours spent on client campaigns, ensuring all billable time is accounted for on invoices.

7. Expense Tracking

- Categorize expenses by project or client to monitor profitability.
- Use the mobile app to capture receipts on the go, linking them to specific clients or projects.

8. Pro Tip:

Set up recurring expenses (e.g., software subscriptions) to save time and ensure accurate budgeting.

9. Invoicing and Payments

- Create detailed invoices that include billable hours, materials, and expenses.
- Offer multiple payment methods to clients, including credit cards and ACH transfers, for convenience.

3. Freelancers: Simplifying Invoicing, Expenses, and Tax Deductions

Freelancers often juggle multiple clients and income streams while managing their own expenses and taxes. QuickBooks Online simplifies these processes, helping freelancers stay organized and focused on their work.

Key Features for Freelancers

1. Simplified Invoicing

- Create professional invoices with your branding and payment terms.
- Set up recurring invoices for regular clients to save time.
- Send automated payment reminders for overdue invoices.

2. How to Customize Invoices:

- Go to the "Invoicing" section and select "Customize."
- Add your logo, adjust the layout, and include personalized notes (e.g., payment instructions).

3. Pro Tip:

- Use the "Invoice Tracker" to monitor payment status and follow up with clients who are late.

4. Expense Categorization

- Track business expenses like travel, software, and office supplies.
- Use predefined categories to simplify tax reporting and maximize deductions.
- Automatically import transactions from linked bank accounts or credit cards.

5. Example Use Case:

A freelance graphic designer can categorize expenses for tools like Adobe Creative Suite under "Software Subscriptions" for easy deduction tracking.

6. Mileage Tracking

- Use the QuickBooks Online mobile app to track mileage automatically or enter it manually.
- Categorize mileage as business or personal for accurate expense reporting.

7. Pro Tip:

Generate a mileage report during tax season to claim deductions for business travel.

8. Tax Preparation

- Use the Self-Employed version of QuickBooks Online for freelancers to estimate quarterly taxes.
- Track 1099 income and prepare forms for contractors if needed.

9. How to Enable Tax Features:

- Go to "Taxes" in the navigation menu.
- Set up estimated tax payments and connect your account to calculate based on income and expenses.

10. Pro Tip:

- Use the "Tax Summary Report" to prepare for year-end filings with minimal hassle.

4. Best Practices for Industry-Specific Customization

While QuickBooks Online offers versatile tools for different industries, adopting best practices ensures you get the most out of the platform:

1. Streamline Your Workflow:

- Automate repetitive tasks like invoicing and expense categorization.
- Use integrations like Shopify for retailers, TSheets for service-based businesses, or PayPal for freelancers.

2. Leverage Reports:

- Retailers: Use sales reports to identify top-performing products.
- Service Providers: Analyze project profitability to focus on high-margin work.
- Freelancers: Track income sources and expense categories to prepare for tax season.

3. Review Settings Regularly:

- Update your inventory, tax rates, or client details periodically to keep your QuickBooks account accurate.

4. Train Your Team (if applicable):

- For retailers or service businesses with staff, train team members on how to use QuickBooks features relevant to their roles.

QuickBooks Online's flexibility and robust feature set make it a powerful tool for businesses of all types. By tailoring the platform to your industry—whether retail, service-based, or freelancing—you can create workflows and processes that save time, improve accuracy, and provide valuable insights into your business's performance.

Understanding how to customize QuickBooks Online for your specific needs ensures you're not only managing your finances effectively but also positioning your business for growth. With a system that aligns perfectly with your operations, you can focus on what you do best: running and growing your business. Let's move on to managing notifications and permissions to keep everything running smoothly and securely.

Managing Notifications and Permissions: Keeping Everything on Track

Managing a business involves juggling multiple tasks, deadlines, and responsibilities, which can make it easy to overlook critical financial activities. QuickBooks Online's notification and permission features are designed to help you stay organized, meet deadlines, and maintain control over your financial data. Notifications ensure you're reminded of essential tasks like sending invoices, reconciling accounts, or paying bills, while permissions allow you to delegate tasks securely and efficiently without compromising sensitive information.

In this chapter, we'll explore how to configure notifications and permissions in QuickBooks Online to keep everything on track.

1. Understanding Notifications in QuickBooks Online

Notifications are alerts that help you stay on top of your financial tasks and ensure you never miss important deadlines. Quick-Books Online provides various notification types tailored to your business needs.

Types of Notifications

1. Invoice and Payment Alerts

- Alerts for overdue invoices.
- Notifications when payments are received.

2. Expense Tracking and Bill Reminders

- Alerts for upcoming and overdue bills.
- Notifications for recurring expenses.

3. Task Alerts

- Reminders for reconciliation deadlines or tax filings.
- Notifications for scheduled reports or bank account updates.

4. Integration Notifications

- Alerts from connected apps, such as inventory updates from Shopify or payment notifications from PayPal.

2. Configuring Notifications

Properly configuring notifications ensures you receive timely alerts for the activities that matter most while avoiding unnecessary distractions.

Step-by-Step Guide to Setting Up Notifications

1. Access Notification Settings

- Click the **Gear Icon** in the upper right corner.
- Select **Notifications** from the dropdown menu.

2. Choose Notification Types

- Browse through available notification options and toggle on/off as needed.
- For example, enable invoice reminders if you often send client invoices but disable recurring expense alerts if you already track them elsewhere.

3. Set Delivery Preferences

- Notifications can be delivered via:
    - **Email:** Ideal for detailed alerts like overdue bills.
    - **Mobile Push Notifications:** Best for quick reminders, like payment confirmations.
    - **In-App Alerts:** Found in the QuickBooks Online dashboard for a central view of all tasks.

4. Customize Frequency

- Adjust notification timing to match your workflow. For example:

- Invoice reminders: Set them to send three days before the due date.
- Bill payment alerts: Receive notifications one week in advance.

Best Practices for Notifications

- Prioritize critical alerts like overdue invoices or upcoming tax deadlines.
- Review notification settings quarterly to ensure they align with your current needs.
- Avoid overloading yourself with alerts to maintain focus on high-priority tasks.

3. Using Notifications to Streamline Workflow

Notifications aren't just reminders—they can become integral tools for optimizing your workflow.

Examples of How Notifications Enhance Efficiency

1. Invoice Tracking

- Receive alerts when a client views an invoice, allowing you to follow up proactively if needed.
- Set reminders for overdue invoices to ensure timely payments.

2. Expense Monitoring

- Enable notifications for large or unexpected expenses to maintain control over cash flow.
- Use alerts for recurring expenses to verify payments and prevent missed deadlines.

3. Tax Preparation

- Configure alerts to remind you of quarterly tax filing deadlines or estimated tax payments.
- Ensure you receive notifications for sales tax updates if applicable.

By using notifications strategically, you can delegate tasks more effectively, prioritize your workload, and maintain better control over your finances.

4. Managing Permissions in QuickBooks Online

While notifications help you stay on track, permissions allow you to securely delegate tasks and manage access to your QuickBooks Online account. Permissions are critical for businesses with multiple users, as they ensure that team members, contractors, or accountants can access only the information and tools relevant to their roles.

Types of User Roles

1. Admin

- Full access to all features and data.
- Ideal for business owners or primary managers.

2. Standard User

- Limited access based on assigned permissions.
- Example: A sales team member may only need access to invoices and customer records.

3. Reports-Only User

- Access to view and generate reports without the ability to edit data.
- Ideal for investors or stakeholders who need financial insights but don't manage daily operations.

4. Time Tracking-Only User

- Access to log hours without interacting with other features.
- Perfect for contractors or hourly employees.

5. Setting Up User Permissions

Configuring permissions ensures data security while allowing team members to contribute effectively.

Step-by-Step Guide to Setting Up Permissions

1. Access User Management

- Navigate to **Settings** and select **Manage Users** under the "Your Company" section.

2. Invite Users

- Click **Add User** and enter the individual's email address.

- Choose the appropriate user role (e.g., Admin, Standard User, Reports Only).

3. Define Permissions for Standard Users

- Select areas the user can access, such as:
  - **Sales and Customers**: For invoicing or payment tracking.
  - **Expenses and Vendors**: For bill management or expense tracking.
  - **Banking**: For reconciling accounts or managing transactions.

4. Review and Confirm

- Before finalizing, review the user's access to ensure it aligns with their responsibilities.
- Click **Send Invite** to provide access.

Adjusting Permissions

- Permissions can be updated at any time by returning to the **Manage Users** menu.
- Regularly review permissions to ensure they remain relevant, especially after personnel changes.

6. Enhancing Security with Permissions

Permissions are not just about efficiency—they're also a key element of protecting sensitive financial data.

Best Practices for Secure Permissions

1. Use the Principle of Least Privilege

- Grant users access to only the features they need. For example, a marketing assistant doesn't require access to bank reconciliations.

2. Monitor User Activity

- QuickBooks Online includes an **Audit Log** that tracks user activity, such as transactions created or edited.
- Regularly review the log to detect unauthorized changes.

3. Restrict Admin Access

- Limit admin roles to a small, trusted group, such as the business owner and a senior accountant.

4. Deactivate Inactive Users

- Remove access for former employees, contractors, or temporary staff who no longer need it.

7. Leveraging Permissions for Collaboration

Permissions enable you to collaborate with your team or external partners without compromising security. For example:

- **Working with an Accountant:**

Assign an admin or accountant role to your CPA, giving them full access to financial data without exposing unrelated business information.

- **Delegating Tasks:**

Allow employees to handle specific tasks, such as invoicing or time tracking, while retaining oversight of the overall system.

- **Sharing Insights:**

Provide stakeholders or investors with reports-only access to keep them informed about your business's financial health.

8. Troubleshooting Notifications and Permissions

Despite best efforts, occasional issues may arise with notifications or permissions. Here's how to address common problems:

1. Missed Notifications

- Check your email's spam folder for alerts.
- Ensure notification settings are enabled and correctly configured.

2. Unauthorized Access

- Use the **Audit Log** to identify unauthorized changes and revoke access immediately.
- Update passwords and enable two-factor authentication for added security.

3. Permission Conflicts

- If a user is unable to access a feature they need, review and adjust their permissions in the **Manage Users** menu.

Notifications and permissions are essential tools for keeping your financial management organized, efficient, and secure. By configuring notifications strategically, you can stay ahead of critical tasks and deadlines, ensuring your business runs smoothly. At the same time, permissions allow you to delegate responsibilities and collaborate effectively without compromising sensitive data.

When used together, these features empower you to maintain control over your business finances while fostering a more productive and secure workflow. With notifications keeping you informed and permissions ensuring safe delegation, you're now ready to explore the essential features of QuickBooks Online for everyday use in the next chapter.

CHAPTER 3

ESSENTIAL FEATURES FOR EVERYDAY USE

Managing the daily financial tasks of your business can be overwhelming without the right tools, but QuickBooks Online is designed to simplify these processes and keep you organized. Whether it's sending invoices, tracking expenses, or managing your bank transactions, mastering these core features will make your day-to-day operations more efficient and less stressful.

This chapter focuses on the **essential features of QuickBooks Online** that every business owner should utilize. First, we'll explore the invoicing tools, which allow you to create professional templates, automate recurring invoices, and track payment statuses. Streamlined invoicing not only ensures you get paid on time but also gives your business a polished, professional image.

Next, we'll dive into **expense tracking**, where you'll learn how to categorize expenses effectively for tax preparation and budgeting. Whether you're recording a one-off purchase or logging recurring bills, QuickBooks Online helps you stay on top of your cash flow and identify areas for cost-saving.

Finally, we'll cover the importance of **connecting your bank accounts**, a feature that automates the import and categorization of transactions. By linking your financial accounts, you can eliminate manual data entry, reduce errors, and get a real-time view of your business's financial health.

By the end of this chapter, you'll have a solid understanding of how to use these essential features to save time, improve accuracy, and maintain control over your finances. Let's get started!

Invoicing Simplified: Professional Templates and Automation Tricks

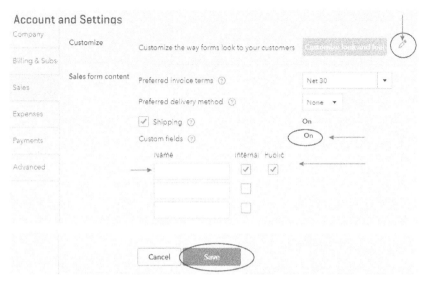

Invoicing is one of the most critical financial tasks for any business. Whether you're a freelancer, a service provider, or a retailer, sending accurate, professional invoices ensures you get paid promptly and maintain strong relationships with your clients. QuickBooks Online streamlines this process by offering tools to create customized templates, automate repetitive tasks, and track payment statuses. In this section, we'll explore how to make the most of QuickBooks Online's invoicing features to save time, reduce errors, and maintain a polished, professional image.

1. Creating Professional Invoice Templates

Your invoices are often the first financial document a client receives, making them an important reflection of your brand. QuickBooks Online allows you to create professional templates that align with your business's identity, enhancing your credibility and ensuring clear communication.

How to Create a Customized Invoice Template

1. **Navigate to the Customization Tool**

- Go to the **Settings** menu (gear icon) and select **Custom Form Styles**.
- Click **New Style** and choose **Invoice**.

2. **Customize the Layout**

- Adjust the layout to suit your business needs:
  - Add or remove fields (e.g., due date, PO number).
  - Rearrange elements for clarity and emphasis.
- Choose a design that reflects your brand, such as modern or traditional styles.

3. **Add Branding**

- Upload your logo and select brand colors to create a cohesive look.
- Use consistent fonts and spacing for a polished, professional appearance.

4. **Include Payment Details**

- Clearly specify payment terms (e.g., net 30, due on receipt).
- Add accepted payment methods like credit cards, PayPal, or ACH transfers.

5. **Save the Template**

- Save your customized invoice template for future use. You can create multiple templates for different purposes, such as project-specific invoices or recurring billing.

Pro Tip: Clarity is Key

Use simple language and concise formatting. Include itemized details of products or services provided, along with their respective costs, to avoid confusion and ensure quick payment.

2. Automating Invoice Processes

Manually creating and sending invoices for recurring services or subscription-based products can be time-consuming. Quick-Books Online's automation tools simplify this by allowing you to set up recurring invoices, automate payment reminders, and streamline follow-ups.

Setting Up Recurring Invoices

Recurring invoices are ideal for businesses with subscription models or repeat customers. For example, a marketing consultant billing clients monthly can automate the invoicing process.

1. **Create a New Invoice**

- Go to the **+ New** menu and select **Invoice**.
- Fill out the invoice details, including the client's information, product/service description, and payment terms.

2. **Enable Recurring Options**

- Before saving, click on **Make Recurring** at the bottom of the invoice.
- Choose the frequency (e.g., weekly, monthly) and set start and end dates.

3. **Customize the Recurrence**

- Select whether to automatically send the invoice or save it as a draft for manual review.

4. **Save and Automate**

- Once saved, QuickBooks Online will generate and send invoices according to the specified schedule.

Automating Payment Reminders

Late payments can disrupt cash flow and add unnecessary stress. QuickBooks Online allows you to send automated payment reminders, encouraging clients to pay on time without requiring manual follow-ups.

1. **Access Reminder Settings**

- Navigate to the **Settings** menu and select **All Lists** under the "Lists" section.
- Choose **Terms** and click on **Edit** next to the payment term you'd like to set reminders for.

2. **Enable Automatic Reminders**

- Configure reminders to send a few days before or after the due date.
- Customize the reminder email to include your branding and a polite request for payment.

3. Track Follow-Ups

- Use the invoice tracking feature to monitor which clients have received reminders and which invoices remain unpaid.

Pro Tip: Be Professional but Firm

Maintain a friendly tone in reminder emails while emphasizing the importance of prompt payment. For example: "Hello [Client Name], we hope you're doing well. This is a friendly reminder that Invoice #1234 is due on [Date]. If you've already made your payment, thank you! If not, please feel free to contact us if you have any questions."

3. Tracking Invoice Status

QuickBooks Online provides robust tools for tracking invoice statuses, ensuring you always know which invoices are outstanding, paid, or overdue. This feature is invaluable for managing cash flow and maintaining financial transparency.

Using the Invoice Tracker

1. Access Invoice Tracker

- Go to the **Sales** tab and select **Invoices**.
- The tracker displays a list of all invoices, categorized by status:
  - **Open**: Sent but unpaid.
  - **Overdue**: Past the due date.
  - **Paid**: Fully settled.
  - **Draft**: Saved but not sent.

2. Monitor Payment Progress

- Check whether clients have viewed the invoice (marked as "Viewed").
- Track partial payments for invoices allowing installments.

3. Send Follow-Ups

- Quickly send payment reminders or follow-up emails directly from the tracker.

Generating Invoice Reports

For a comprehensive overview, generate invoice reports that provide insights into your receivables.

1. **Go to the Reports Section**
- Navigate to **Reports** and search for "Invoice List" or "Aging Summary."

2. **Customize Filters**
- Filter by date range, customer, or status to focus on specific invoices.

3. **Analyze Data**
- Use these reports to identify payment trends, such as consistently late-paying clients or seasonal fluctuations in receivables.

4. Offering Multiple Payment Options

Providing clients with convenient payment methods can significantly reduce the time it takes to receive payment. QuickBooks Online integrates with various payment processors to streamline this process.

Integrating Payment Options

1. **Enable QuickBooks Payments**
- Go to **Settings** and select **Payments**.
- Enable QuickBooks Payments to allow clients to pay directly through the invoice.

2. **Add Payment Methods**
- Link payment processors like PayPal, Stripe, or credit card gateways.
- Specify accepted payment methods on each invoice.

3. **Track Payment Status**
- Payments made through QuickBooks Payments are automatically updated in your account.

Pro Tip: Incentivize Early Payments

Offer small discounts for clients who pay early, and clearly indicate these terms on the invoice. For example: "2% discount if paid within 10 days."

5. Best Practices for Effective Invoicing

Invoicing is more than just sending bills—it's about fostering clear communication and ensuring smooth financial transactions. Here are some best practices:

1. **Set Clear Payment Terms**

- Specify payment deadlines, late fees, and accepted payment methods on all invoices.

2. **Send Invoices Promptly**

- Avoid delays in billing by sending invoices as soon as services are rendered or products are delivered.

3. **Double-Check Details**

- Review invoices for accuracy before sending, ensuring that quantities, prices, and client information are correct.

4. **Follow Up Regularly**

- Use automated reminders or set calendar alerts to follow up on overdue invoices.

5. **Maintain Professionalism**

- Use branded templates and clear language to convey professionalism.

QuickBooks Online's invoicing tools empower you to manage one of the most critical aspects of your business with ease and efficiency. From creating professional templates to automating recurring invoices and tracking payment statuses, these features save time, reduce errors, and help you maintain a strong cash flow. By implementing best practices and leveraging QuickBooks Online's robust capabilities, you can simplify your invoicing process and ensure you get paid promptly. Now that you're equipped to handle invoicing like a pro, let's explore how to manage expenses effectively in the next section.

Tracking Expenses: Categorization for Tax and Budget Management

Expense tracking is a fundamental aspect of financial management, helping businesses monitor cash flow, stay on top of spending, and prepare for tax season. QuickBooks Online simplifies this process by providing tools to categorize expenses, automate tracking, and generate reports that give you a clear picture of where your money is going. Effective expense tracking not only ensures accurate financial records but also helps you optimize your budget and maximize tax deductions.

In this section, we'll explore how to use QuickBooks Online to track, categorize, and manage expenses effectively.

1. The Importance of Expense Tracking

Keeping a detailed record of your business expenses is critical for several reasons:

1.   **Cash Flow Management**

- Monitoring expenses ensures you don't overspend and helps you identify unnecessary costs.
- Real-time visibility into expenses allows you to adjust spending when necessary.

2.   **Tax Preparation**

- Properly categorized expenses simplify tax filing and help you claim deductions.
- Accurate expense records provide proof in case of an audit.

3.   **Budgeting and Financial Planning**

- Analyzing expense data enables you to set realistic budgets and identify cost-saving opportunities.
- Tracking trends over time helps you plan for future investments.

By using QuickBooks Online to manage expenses, you can automate much of this process, saving time and reducing errors.

2. Recording Expenses in QuickBooks Online

QuickBooks Online allows you to record expenses manually or automate the process by linking your financial accounts.

Manually Entering Expenses

1. **Go to the Expense Tab**

- Click on **Expenses** in the left-hand menu, then select **New Transaction** > **Expense**.

2. **Fill Out Expense Details**

- Enter the date, amount, and vendor.
- Choose the payment method (e.g., credit card, bank transfer, cash).

3. **Categorize the Expense**

- Select an appropriate category from the dropdown menu, such as "Office Supplies," "Advertising," or "Travel."
- Add a memo for additional context, like "Client meeting lunch" or "Software subscription."

4. **Save and Close**

- Review the details for accuracy before saving the transaction.

Capturing Receipts on the Go

QuickBooks Online's mobile app allows you to snap photos of receipts and upload them directly to your account.

1. **Open the QuickBooks App**

- Navigate to the receipt capture feature.

2. **Upload the Receipt**

- Take a photo of the receipt or upload an existing image.

- QuickBooks will attempt to extract key details (e.g., amount, date, vendor).

3. Categorize and Match
- Assign the receipt to an expense category and match it to a recorded transaction, if applicable.

3. Automating Expense Tracking

Automation can save significant time and ensure accuracy in expense tracking. QuickBooks Online provides several tools for automating this process:

Linking Bank and Credit Card Accounts

By connecting your financial accounts to QuickBooks Online, transactions are automatically imported and categorized.

1. Navigate to the Banking Tab
- Click **Banking** in the left-hand menu, then select **Link Account**.

2. Connect Your Account
- Choose your bank or credit card provider and log in using your credentials.
- Select the accounts you want to link (e.g., business checking, company credit card).

3. Set Up Rules for Categorization
- Create rules for recurring transactions. For example:
  - "Categorize all payments to Zoom as 'Software Subscriptions.'"
  - "Assign all Amazon purchases to 'Office Supplies.'"

Recurring Transactions

QuickBooks Online allows you to set up recurring expenses for predictable costs, such as rent or subscriptions.

1. Create a New Recurring Expense
- Go to **+ New**, select **Expense**, and fill in the details.

2. Enable Recurrence

- Choose the frequency (e.g., monthly, weekly) and start/end dates.

3. **Save and Automate**

- Once saved, QuickBooks will automatically record the transaction on the specified schedule.

4. Categorizing Expenses for Tax Management

Proper categorization is crucial for tax preparation. QuickBooks Online includes predefined categories that align with common tax deductions, ensuring you don't miss out on savings.

Common Expense Categories

1. **Office Expenses**

- Office supplies, utilities, and rent.

2. **Travel**

- Flights, hotels, meals, and transportation for business purposes.

3. **Marketing and Advertising**

- Social media ads, website hosting, and promotional materials.

4. **Professional Services**

- Accountant fees, consulting services, or legal expenses.

5. **Software and Subscriptions**

- SaaS tools like QuickBooks, Adobe Creative Suite, or Zoom.

6. **Employee Wages and Benefits**

- Payroll costs, health insurance, and retirement contributions.

How to Categorize Expenses in QuickBooks Online

1. **Choose a Category**

- When recording an expense, select the most relevant category from the dropdown menu.

2. **Add Subcategories (if needed)**

- For example, create subcategories under "Travel" for "Flights" and "Hotel Stays."

3. Use Tags for Specific Tracking

- Tags allow you to group transactions for non-standard tracking purposes, like events or campaigns.

5. Generating Expense Reports

Expense reports provide a comprehensive view of your spending, helping you make data-driven decisions and prepare for taxes.

Creating an Expense Report

1. Navigate to Reports

- Go to the **Reports** tab in the left-hand menu.

2. Choose a Report Template

- Select templates like "Expense by Vendor Summary" or "Profit and Loss."

3. Customize Filters

- Adjust the date range, vendor, or category to focus on specific expenses.

4. Run the Report

- Generate the report and export it as a PDF or Excel file for review.

Interpreting Expense Reports

1. Identify Spending Patterns

- Look for trends, such as seasonal fluctuations or overspending in certain categories.

2. Evaluate Vendor Relationships

- Analyze spending by vendor to assess cost-effectiveness or negotiate better terms.

3. Plan for Tax Season

- Use categorized expenses to calculate deductions and estimate your tax liability.

6. Budgeting with Expense Data

Tracking expenses in QuickBooks Online also enables effective budgeting. By analyzing historical data, you can set realistic spending limits and allocate resources more efficiently.

How to Create a Budget

1. **Access the Budgeting Tool**
- Go to the **Settings** menu and select **Budgets**.
2. **Set Parameters**
- Define the budget's duration (monthly, quarterly, annually) and categories.
3. **Input Historical Data**
- Use past expense reports to establish baseline figures for each category.
4. **Monitor Performance**
- Compare actual spending to budgeted amounts using the Budget vs. Actual report.

Pro Tip: Adjust Budgets Regularly

Review your budget quarterly and make adjustments based on changes in revenue, expenses, or business priorities.

7. Avoiding Common Expense Tracking Mistakes

1. **Failing to Record Small Transactions**
- Even minor expenses, like parking fees or office snacks, add up over time. Use the mobile app to capture them on the spot.
2. **Misclassifying Expenses**
- Ensure expenses are assigned to the correct category to avoid confusion during tax preparation.
3. **Not Reconciling Accounts**
- Regularly reconcile your bank and credit card accounts to catch discrepancies early.

Tracking expenses effectively is essential for maintaining financial health, optimizing budgets, and preparing for tax season. Quick-

Books Online simplifies this process with tools for automation, categorization, and reporting, making it easy to stay organized and make informed decisions. By leveraging these features, you can minimize errors, maximize tax deductions, and gain valuable insights into your spending patterns.

With your expenses under control, you're one step closer to mastering your business finances. Let's move on to the next section, where we'll explore how to connect your bank accounts to automate data imports and ensure seamless updates.

Connecting Bank Accounts: Automating Data Import for Seamless Updates

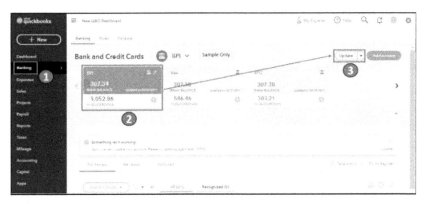

Managing financial transactions manually can be time-consuming, error-prone, and overwhelming. QuickBooks Online solves this challenge by allowing you to connect your bank accounts and credit cards directly to the platform. This feature automates the import of transaction data, ensuring your financial records are always up-to-date without the need for constant manual input. By connecting your accounts, you can save time, reduce errors, and gain real-time insights into your business's financial health.

In this section, we'll walk you through the process of connecting your bank accounts to QuickBooks Online, explain how to automate data imports, and highlight best practices for managing your transactions efficiently.

1. Benefits of Connecting Bank Accounts

Linking your bank accounts and credit cards to QuickBooks Online offers numerous advantages for your business:

1.1. Automation Saves Time

- Transactions are automatically imported, eliminating the need for manual entry.
- Rules can be applied to categorize recurring expenses and income, streamlining workflows.

1.2. Enhanced Accuracy

- Direct bank feeds reduce the likelihood of errors associated with manual input.
- Matching transactions ensures consistency between your bank statements and financial records.

1.3. Real-Time Financial Updates

- Stay informed about your cash flow with up-to-date data on income, expenses, and balances.
- Quickly identify trends or irregularities that may require attention.

1.4. Simplified Reconciliation

- Automatically imported transactions simplify the reconciliation process, ensuring your books are balanced with minimal effort.

2. Connecting Your Bank Accounts to QuickBooks Online

The process of linking your bank accounts is straightforward and can be completed in just a few steps. QuickBooks Online supports connections with most major banks and credit card providers, making it easy to integrate your financial accounts.

Step-by-Step Guide to Linking Accounts

1. **Navigate to the Banking Section**

- From the QuickBooks Online dashboard, click on the **Banking** tab in the left-hand menu.

2. Start the Connection Process

- Click the **Link Account** button at the top right of the Banking page.

3. Select Your Bank

- Use the search bar to find your bank or credit card provider. QuickBooks Online supports a wide range of institutions, from large national banks to regional credit unions.

4. Log In to Your Bank Account

- Enter your online banking credentials. QuickBooks Online will establish a secure connection to your account.

5. Choose the Accounts to Connect

- Select which accounts you'd like to link (e.g., checking, savings, or credit card).
- Assign each account to the appropriate category in Quick-Books, such as business checking or company credit card.

6. Set the Transaction Import Range

- Specify how far back you'd like QuickBooks to import transactions (e.g., the past 30 or 90 days).

7. Review and Confirm

- Verify the details and confirm the connection. Once complete, your transactions will begin importing automatically.

Security Considerations

QuickBooks Online uses bank-level encryption to protect your financial data. Two-factor authentication (2FA) is often required by your bank to add an extra layer of security during the connection process.

3. Managing Transactions After Import

Once your bank accounts are connected, QuickBooks Online will begin importing transactions. These transactions will appear in the **For Review** tab under the Banking section, where you can categorize, match, or exclude them.

3.1. Categorizing Transactions

Proper categorization is essential for accurate financial reporting and tax preparation.

1. Assign Categories

- Select a transaction and choose a category from the drop-down menu (e.g., "Office Supplies," "Travel," or "Advertising").
- Use QuickBooks' predefined categories or create custom ones tailored to your business.

2. Add Details

- Include a memo or tag for additional context, such as "Client lunch" or "Monthly software subscription."

3. Split Transactions

- For transactions covering multiple categories, use the **Split** option to allocate amounts accordingly.

3.2. Matching Transactions

QuickBooks Online attempts to match imported transactions with those you've already recorded, such as invoices or bill payments.

1. Review Suggested Matches

- Matches will be highlighted in green with a "Match Found" label.

2. Confirm or Edit

- Click on the transaction to review the details. If correct, select **Match** to reconcile it. If not, adjust the transaction before matching.

3.3. Excluding Transactions

Occasionally, duplicate or irrelevant transactions may appear.

1. Identify Unnecessary Entries

- Select transactions that don't belong in your financial records (e.g., personal expenses accidentally charged to a business card).

2. Exclude Transactions

- Use the **Exclude** option to remove these entries from your bookkeeping without deleting them entirely.

4. Automating Transaction Categorization

QuickBooks Online allows you to create rules for recurring transactions, automating categorization and saving time.

How to Create Rules

1. **Access Banking Rules**
- Go to the **Banking** section and click on **Rules** at the top right.

2. **Set Conditions**
- Define the criteria for the rule, such as:
   - **Description Contains:** Specify keywords (e.g., "Amazon" for office supplies).
   - **Amount Is Greater/Less Than:** Set thresholds for categorization.

3. **Choose an Action**
- Assign a category (e.g., "Marketing" for Facebook Ads).
- Select additional actions, like adding a memo or splitting the transaction.

4. **Save the Rule**
- Once created, QuickBooks Online will automatically apply the rule to future transactions that meet the criteria.

5. Reconciling Accounts for Accuracy

Reconciliation ensures that your QuickBooks Online records match your bank statements. By reconciling regularly, you can catch errors or discrepancies early.

How to Reconcile Accounts

1. **Go to the Reconciliation Tool**
- Click on the **Accounting** tab and select **Reconcile.**

2. **Select an Account**
- Choose the bank account or credit card you'd like to reconcile.

3. **Enter Statement Details**
- Input the ending balance and date from your bank statement.

4. **Match Transactions**

- Review the list of transactions in QuickBooks and check them off as you match them to your statement.

5. Resolve Discrepancies

- If there's a discrepancy, look for missing or duplicate transactions and adjust as needed.

6. Finalize the Reconciliation

- Once all transactions are matched, click **Finish Now** to complete the process.

Pro Tip: Reconcile Monthly

Reconcile your accounts at least once a month to maintain accurate financial records and streamline tax preparation.

6. Best Practices for Managing Connected Accounts

To get the most out of your connected accounts, follow these best practices:

1. Regularly Review Transactions

- Check the **For Review** tab weekly to ensure all transactions are categorized or matched promptly.

2. Keep Business and Personal Accounts Separate

- Avoid mixing personal and business expenses by using dedicated accounts for your business.

3. Monitor for Errors

- Occasionally, bank feeds may import incorrect data. Review transactions carefully to catch and correct any issues.

4. Use Bank Feed Reports

- Generate reports to analyze imported transactions and identify trends in spending or income.

7. Troubleshooting Connection Issues

Sometimes, bank connections may encounter issues due to updates or outages. Here's how to troubleshoot common problems:

1. Reconnect Your Account

- If transactions stop syncing, try disconnecting and reconnecting the account.

2. Check Bank Status

- Verify that your bank isn't experiencing downtime or maintenance.

3. Contact Support

- QuickBooks Online provides customer support to resolve persistent connection issues.

Connecting your bank accounts to QuickBooks Online is a game-changer for efficient financial management. By automating data imports, categorizing transactions, and reconciling accounts, you can save time, reduce errors, and maintain up-to-date financial records. This seamless integration provides real-time insights into your business's financial health, empowering you to make informed decisions and focus on growing your business.

With your bank accounts successfully connected and transactions managed, you're now ready to explore the next steps in organizing your finances, such as generating key financial reports and preparing for tax season. Let's continue optimizing your QuickBooks Online experience!

CHAPTER 4

MONTHLY CHECKLISTS FOR ORGANIZED FINANCES

Keeping your finances organized is essential for maintaining a healthy business, and monthly checklists are a powerful tool for staying on top of key tasks. By following a consistent process each month, you can ensure that your financial records are accurate, your reports are meaningful, and your business is well-prepared for tax season.

In this chapter, we'll guide you through three critical monthly tasks: reconciling accounts, generating key financial reports, and closing the books. First, we'll explore the importance of **account reconciliation**, which ensures that your financial records align with your bank and credit card statements. This process not only identifies discrepancies but also helps you catch potential errors or fraud early.

Next, we'll dive into **generating financial reports**, including the Profit & Loss statement, Balance Sheet, and Cash Flow report. These reports provide valuable insights into your business's performance, helping you make informed decisions about growth, spending, and investment.

Finally, we'll cover the steps for **closing the books**, a process that locks in your financial data for the month and prepares you for tax season. By following these steps, you can maintain clean, accurate records that make year-end reporting and tax filing much easier.

With this monthly checklist in place, you'll gain better control over your finances, reduce stress, and ensure your business stays on track for success. Let's get started!

Reconciling Accounts: Ensuring Accurate Financial Records

Reconciling accounts is one of the most important tasks for maintaining accurate financial records and ensuring your books align with reality. It involves comparing your financial records in QuickBooks Online with your bank and credit card statements to ensure every transaction matches. Regular reconciliation helps you catch errors, detect fraud, and maintain confidence in your financial data.

In this section, we'll dive into the purpose of account reconciliation, the step-by-step process in QuickBooks Online, and best practices for maintaining accurate records.

1. Why Reconciliation Matters

Reconciling your accounts isn't just a bookkeeping task; it's a fundamental practice for ensuring the integrity of your financial data. Here's why it's crucial:

1.1. Detecting Errors

Mistakes happen, whether it's a duplicate entry, a missed transaction, or a typo in the amount recorded. Reconciling allows you to identify and correct these errors promptly.

1.2. Preventing Fraud

Regularly comparing your records with bank and credit card statements helps you spot unauthorized transactions or fraudulent activity early.

1.3. Ensuring Tax Compliance

Accurate records are essential for preparing tax filings. Reconciliation ensures that your financial data is complete and consistent, reducing the risk of audits or penalties.

1.4. Improving Decision-Making

Accurate, up-to-date financial records give you a clear picture of your business's cash flow and financial health, helping you make better strategic decisions.

2. Preparing for Reconciliation

Before you begin reconciling accounts in QuickBooks Online, it's essential to gather the necessary information and ensure your setup is correct.

2.1. Gather Bank and Credit Card Statements

Collect the monthly statements for the accounts you'll be reconciling. These statements provide the starting and ending balances, as well as the transactions to compare against your QuickBooks records.

2.2. Review Transactions

Ensure that all transactions for the period have been entered into QuickBooks, whether manually or through automated bank feeds. Common transactions to check include:

- Invoices and customer payments.
- Expenses and bill payments.
- Transfers between accounts.

2.3. Resolve Outstanding Items

Address any uncleared or outstanding items from previous reconciliations before starting the new period.

3. How to Reconcile Accounts in QuickBooks Online

QuickBooks Online provides an intuitive reconciliation tool that simplifies the process. Follow these steps to reconcile your accounts:

Step 1: Access the Reconciliation Tool

- Log in to QuickBooks Online.
- Navigate to the **Accounting** menu and select **Reconcile**.

Step 2: Choose an Account

- Select the bank or credit card account you want to reconcile from the dropdown list.

Step 3: Enter Statement Information

- Input the **Ending Balance** and **Statement Ending Date** from your bank or credit card statement.
- Double-check the beginning balance in QuickBooks to ensure it matches the ending balance from your last reconciliation.

Step 4: Match Transactions

QuickBooks Online will display a list of transactions for the selected account. Your goal is to match these transactions with those on your statement.

- **Check Off Matching Transactions**: Compare each transaction in QuickBooks with the corresponding entry on your statement. Check the box next to each matching transaction.
- **Identify Discrepancies**: If a transaction doesn't match or is missing, investigate further. Look for errors such as incorrect amounts, missing entries, or duplicate transactions.

Step 5: Resolve Discrepancies

- **Edit Transactions**: If a transaction amount is incorrect, click on it to make corrections.
- **Add Missing Transactions**: Use the **+ New** menu to record any transactions that were omitted.
- **Exclude Irrelevant Transactions**: If a transaction shouldn't be included, exclude it from the reconciliation.

Step 6: Achieve Zero Difference

The reconciliation tool will display a running total of the difference between your QuickBooks records and your statement. Your goal is to bring this difference to **$0.00**.

Step 7: Finalize the Reconciliation

Once the difference is zero, click **Finish Now** to complete the reconciliation. QuickBooks will lock the reconciled transactions, ensuring they aren't accidentally altered in the future.

4. Handling Common Reconciliation Challenges

Reconciliation isn't always straightforward. Here's how to handle some common challenges:

4.1. Missing Transactions

If a transaction appears on your statement but not in QuickBooks:

- Check for a manual error or missing data.
- Add the transaction to QuickBooks and assign it to the correct category.

4.2. Duplicate Transactions

If a transaction is recorded twice in QuickBooks:

- Use the **Find Match** feature to locate and merge duplicates.
- Exclude or delete the duplicate entry.

4.3. Incorrect Beginning Balance

If the beginning balance in QuickBooks doesn't match your statement:

- Review the reconciliation history to identify discrepancies from previous periods.
- Adjust balances as needed, ensuring that changes are documented.

4.4. Uncleared Transactions

Uncleared transactions from prior periods can complicate reconciliation:

- Verify whether these transactions should be voided or carried forward.
- Follow up with banks or vendors to confirm unresolved items.

5. Best Practices for Accurate Reconciliation

Consistency and attention to detail are key to successful reconciliation. Follow these best practices to ensure accuracy:

5.1. Reconcile Monthly

- Reconcile accounts at the end of each month to stay current and reduce the workload for year-end reviews.

5.2. Keep Supporting Documentation

- Retain bank statements, invoices, and receipts for every transaction. This documentation is invaluable for audits or resolving disputes.

5.3. Use Automated Bank Feeds

- Link your bank accounts to QuickBooks Online to automate transaction imports and reduce manual entry errors.

5.4. Regularly Review the Audit Log

- QuickBooks Online includes an **Audit Log** that tracks changes to transactions. Regularly review this log to identify unauthorized edits or suspicious activity.

5.5. Work with Your Accountant

- If reconciliation becomes complex, collaborate with your accountant or bookkeeper to ensure your records are accurate.

6. Benefits of Regular Reconciliation

By making reconciliation a monthly habit, you can enjoy several benefits:

1. **Improved Financial Visibility**

- Accurate records provide a clear picture of your cash flow, enabling better decision-making.

2. **Reduced Stress During Tax Season**
- Clean, reconciled records simplify tax preparation and reduce the risk of errors.

3. **Early Detection of Issues**
- Regular reviews help you catch and address discrepancies, fraud, or unauthorized transactions quickly.

4. **Stronger Business Credibility**
- Accurate financial records build trust with stakeholders, including investors, lenders, and auditors.

7. Reconciling Multiple Accounts

If you manage multiple bank or credit card accounts, QuickBooks Online allows you to reconcile each account separately. Use the same process for each account, ensuring consistency across your financial records.

8. Troubleshooting Reconciliation Issues

If reconciliation doesn't balance despite your best efforts, here's what to do:

- **Use the Reconciliation Report**: Generate a reconciliation report to identify specific discrepancies.
- **Review Prior Periods**: Check previous reconciliations for adjustments or errors that could impact the current period.
- **Contact Support**: QuickBooks Online offers customer support and a community forum where you can seek assistance for complex issues.

Reconciling your accounts is a vital step in maintaining accurate financial records and ensuring the integrity of your business's data. With QuickBooks Online's powerful reconciliation tools, you can streamline the process, identify discrepancies, and stay on top of your finances. By making reconciliation a regular part of your monthly workflow, you'll gain confidence in your records, reduce the risk of errors, and set your business up for long-term success.

With your accounts reconciled, you're ready to move on to generating key financial reports to analyze your business's performance and plan for the future. Let's explore that in the next section!

Generating Key Financial Reports: Profit & Loss, Balance Sheet, and More

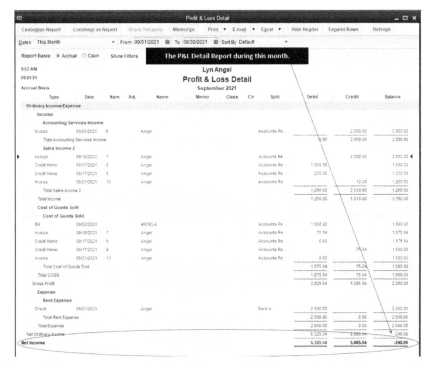

Financial reports are the backbone of informed decision-making for any business. They provide a clear picture of your financial health, help you assess performance, and guide you in setting goals for the future. QuickBooks Online simplifies the process of generating key financial reports, such as the **Profit & Loss (P&L) statement**, **Balance Sheet**, and **Cash Flow statement**, along with other insightful reports tailored to your needs.

In this section, we'll delve into the purpose and importance of these reports, walk you through generating them in QuickBooks Online, and explore how to analyze and use them to drive your business forward.

1. Understanding Key Financial Reports

1.1. Profit & Loss Statement (P&L)

Also known as the Income Statement, the P&L report summarizes your revenue, costs, and expenses over a specified period. It calculates your net profit or loss, giving you a snapshot of your business's profitability.

- **Why It's Important**:
- Shows whether your business is making or losing money.
- Helps identify trends in income and expenses.
- Guides budgeting and cost-cutting decisions.

1.2. Balance Sheet

The Balance Sheet provides a snapshot of your business's financial position at a specific point in time, detailing your assets, liabilities, and equity.

- **Why It's Important**:
- Offers a complete view of your financial health.
- Helps assess liquidity and solvency.
- Serves as a key document for investors and lenders.

1.3. Cash Flow Statement

This report tracks the movement of money in and out of your business, dividing cash flow into operating, investing, and financing activities.

- **Why It's Important**:
- Shows whether your business has enough cash to meet its obligations.
- Highlights areas where cash flow can be improved.
- Helps you prepare for future cash needs.

1.4. Other Useful Reports

- **Accounts Receivable (A/R) Aging Summary**: Tracks outstanding invoices and overdue payments.
- **Accounts Payable (A/P) Aging Summary**: Monitors unpaid bills and upcoming due dates.
- **Sales by Product/Service**: Breaks down revenue by products or services sold.

- **Expense by Vendor Summary**: Highlights spending patterns with vendors.

2. Generating Financial Reports in QuickBooks Online

QuickBooks Online makes it easy to generate detailed financial reports tailored to your business needs. Here's how to create and customize these key reports.

2.1. Accessing Reports

1. **Navigate to the Reports Menu**
- From the dashboard, click on **Reports** in the left-hand menu.

2. **Browse Report Categories**
- QuickBooks organizes reports into categories like "Business Overview," "Sales," "Expenses," and "Taxes."

3. **Search for a Specific Report**
- Use the search bar at the top to quickly find a report, such as "Profit and Loss" or "Balance Sheet."

2.2. Creating the Profit & Loss Report

1. **Select Profit & Loss**
- Click on **Profit and Loss** under the "Business Overview" section.

2. **Set the Date Range**
- Choose a time frame (e.g., monthly, quarterly, or yearly) to analyze performance over that period.

3. **Customize Columns**
- Compare results by month, quarter, or year to identify trends.

4. **Filter by Customer, Product, or Class**
- Use filters to narrow down the data and analyze specific areas of your business.

5. **Run the Report**
- Click **Run Report** to generate the P&L statement.

2.3. Creating the Balance Sheet

1.   Select Balance Sheet

* Find the Balance Sheet report under the "Business Overview" section.

2.   Choose the Date

* Set the report date to reflect your financial position as of a specific day.

3.   Customize the Layout

* Adjust how assets, liabilities, and equity are grouped for clarity.

4.   Run the Report

* Click **Run Report** to view your current financial standing.

2.4. Creating the Cash Flow Statement

1.   Select Statement of Cash Flows

* Locate this report in the "Business Overview" section.

2.   Choose the Period

* Define the period to analyze (e.g., last month, last quarter).

3.   Adjust Presentation

* Decide whether to present cash flow on a direct or indirect basis, depending on your accounting needs.

4.   Run the Report

* Click **Run Report** to generate the cash flow analysis.

2.5. Customizing Reports

QuickBooks Online allows extensive customization to tailor reports to your specific needs.

1.   Use the Customize Button

* Add or remove columns, adjust date ranges, and apply filters.

2.   Save Custom Reports

* Save your customized report settings for future use by clicking **Save Customization**.

3.   Group Reports

- Combine multiple reports into a single group for easy access.

4. **Export Reports**

- Download reports as PDF or Excel files for sharing or additional analysis.

3. Analyzing Financial Reports

Generating reports is just the first step—understanding and interpreting them is where the real value lies.

3.1. Profit & Loss Analysis

- **Compare Revenue and Expenses**: Identify periods with higher profits or losses and investigate the causes.
- **Track Seasonal Trends**: Determine whether certain months or quarters consistently perform better.
- **Monitor Expense Categories**: Look for categories with excessive or unexpected spending.

3.2. Balance Sheet Analysis

- **Assess Liquidity**: Compare current assets to current liabilities to gauge your ability to cover short-term obligations.
- **Monitor Debt Levels**: Track how much of your assets are financed by liabilities versus equity.

3.3. Cash Flow Analysis

- **Identify Cash Gaps**: Pinpoint periods where outflows exceed inflows, signaling potential cash flow issues.
- **Evaluate Investment Activities**: Review cash spent on purchasing equipment or other long-term investments.
- **Monitor Financing Activities**: Assess how much cash is raised through loans or equity and ensure it aligns with your business goals.

4. Using Reports for Decision-Making

Accurate financial reports enable you to make informed decisions that drive your business forward.

4.1. Budgeting and Forecasting

- Use historical data from P&L and Cash Flow reports to set realistic budgets and forecasts.

4.2. Expense Management

- Analyze Expense by Vendor reports to identify cost-saving opportunities or renegotiate vendor contracts.

4.3. Sales Strategies

- Generate Sales by Product/Service reports to determine your most profitable offerings and focus your marketing efforts accordingly.

4.4. Securing Financing

- Provide lenders or investors with Balance Sheets and P&L statements to demonstrate your financial health and growth potential.

5. Best Practices for Report Management

1. **Generate Reports Regularly**
- Run key reports monthly to track progress and address issues promptly.

2. **Save Historical Data**
- Archive reports for future reference, audits, or trend analysis.

3. **Share Reports with Stakeholders**
- Keep team members, investors, and advisors informed by sharing relevant reports.

4. **Integrate with Other Tools**
- Export reports to Excel for deeper analysis or integrate Quick-Books with analytics software for advanced insights.

6. Troubleshooting Common Report Issues

1. **Discrepancies in Reports**
- Verify that all transactions are categorized correctly and accounts are reconciled.

2. **Missing Data**
- Ensure all income and expenses have been entered or imported into QuickBooks.

3. **Formatting Challenges**
- Use the customization tools to adjust formatting and ensure clarity.

Financial reports are essential for understanding your business's performance and planning for the future. QuickBooks Online's robust reporting tools make it easy to generate, customize, and analyze key financial documents, such as the Profit & Loss statement, Balance Sheet, and Cash Flow statement. By leveraging these reports, you can gain valuable insights, make data-driven decisions, and confidently lead your business toward success.

Now that you've mastered generating and analyzing reports, it's time to explore the final step in monthly financial management: closing the books. Let's dive into that process next!

Closing the Books: Preparing Your Finances for Tax Season

Closing the books is a critical monthly process that ensures your financial records are accurate, complete, and ready for tax season or any financial review. It involves finalizing your financial data for a specific period, locking in transactions to prevent changes, and generating reports to prepare for taxes. By implementing a consistent and thorough closing process, you can reduce errors, improve financial visibility, and minimize stress when tax deadlines approach.

In this section, we'll explore the steps to close your books in QuickBooks Online, explain its importance for tax preparation, and share best practices for maintaining clean and accurate records.

1. Why Closing the Books Matters

Closing the books is not just about preparing for tax season; it's an essential part of maintaining organized and reliable financial records. Here's why it's important:

1.1. Locks in Financial Data

- Prevents accidental edits or deletions of finalized transactions, maintaining data integrity.

1.2. Ensures Accurate Reporting

- Guarantees that financial statements, such as the Profit & Loss statement and Balance Sheet, reflect accurate data for the period.

1.3. Simplifies Tax Preparation

- Consolidates your financial information, making it easier to calculate taxable income, deductions, and liabilities.

1.4. Improves Decision-Making

- Provides a clear and finalized picture of your business's financial health, helping you plan for the future.

2. Preparing to Close the Books

Before you officially close your books, there are several preparatory steps to ensure all financial data is accurate and complete.

2.1. Reconcile Your Accounts

Reconciliation ensures that your QuickBooks Online records match your bank and credit card statements. Unreconciled transactions can lead to discrepancies in your reports.

1. Go to **Accounting > Reconcile** in QuickBooks Online.
2. Match all transactions to your bank and credit card statements.
3. Resolve discrepancies, such as missing or duplicate entries.

2.2. Review Outstanding Invoices

1. Navigate to **Sales > Invoices** to check for unpaid invoices.
2. Follow up on overdue payments by sending reminders or contacting customers.
3. Write off bad debts if necessary, categorizing them appropriately for tax purposes.

2.3. Verify Vendor Bills

1. Check **Expenses > Bills** to ensure all vendor bills are recorded and categorized correctly.
2. Mark bills as paid if payments have been issued.

2.4. Categorize All Transactions

1. Use the **Banking > For Review** section to ensure all transactions are categorized.
2. Review uncategorized transactions and assign appropriate categories, such as "Office Supplies" or "Marketing."

2.5. Review Payroll and Employee Expenses

1. Ensure all payroll transactions are recorded and categorized under "Wages" or similar accounts.
2. Verify that employee reimbursements are documented accurately.

2.6. Generate Key Financial Reports

Run a Profit & Loss statement, Balance Sheet, and Cash Flow report for the period to identify any anomalies or missing data.

3. Closing the Books in QuickBooks Online

Once you've prepared your financial data, it's time to officially close the books in QuickBooks Online. This process locks your records for the period, ensuring they remain accurate and tamper-proof.

Step-by-Step Guide to Closing the Books

1. **Access the Account and Settings Menu**

- Go to the **Settings (Gear Icon)** in the top right corner.
- Select **Accounts and Settings** under the "Your Company" section.

2. **Navigate to the Advanced Tab**

- Click on the **Advanced** tab in the left-hand menu.

3. **Enable Closing the Books**

- Scroll to the "Accounting" section and toggle on the **Close the Books** option.

4. **Set a Closing Date**
- Enter the last day of the period you're closing (e.g., the last day of the month or year).

5. **Add a Password**
- Create a password to protect the closed period, ensuring only authorized users can make changes if necessary.

6. **Save Changes**
- Click **Save and Done** to finalize the process.

4. Preparing for Tax Season

Closing the books is an integral part of tax preparation. Here's how to ensure your business is ready for tax season:

4.1. Organize Tax Documents
- Gather all necessary documents, including:
- Profit & Loss statement for taxable income.
- Balance Sheet for assets and liabilities.
- Payroll summaries and 1099 forms for contractors.
- Receipts and invoices for deductible expenses.

4.2. Identify Deductions

Review your expense categories to maximize deductions:
- **Office Supplies and Utilities**: Pens, paper, electricity, internet, etc.
- **Travel and Meals**: Business-related flights, lodging, and meals.
- **Software and Subscriptions**: SaaS tools like QuickBooks or Adobe Creative Suite.
- **Employee Wages and Benefits**: Salaries, bonuses, and healthcare contributions.

4.3. Review Estimated Taxes

If you pay quarterly taxes, ensure that your estimated tax payments match your actual liability for the period.

4.4. Consult with a Tax Professional

Collaborate with a CPA or tax advisor to review your financial data and ensure compliance with tax laws.

5. Common Challenges in Closing the Books

Closing the books can be straightforward with proper preparation, but challenges may still arise. Here's how to address common issues:

5.1. Unreconciled Transactions

- **Solution**: Double-check your bank and credit card statements for missing or incorrect entries. Match transactions carefully.

5.2. Misclassified Expenses

- **Solution**: Review all transactions to ensure they're categorized correctly. Use the **Reclassify Transactions** tool in QuickBooks if needed.

5.3. Incomplete Records

- **Solution**: Run a **Transaction Detail Report** to identify gaps or missing data.

5.4. Adjustments and Journal Entries

- **Solution**: Make journal entries for adjustments, such as depreciation or accruals, with the guidance of an accountant.

6. Best Practices for Closing the Books

1. **Close Monthly**

- Closing the books monthly helps you stay organized and reduces the workload at year-end.

2. **Maintain Supporting Documents**

- Keep copies of bank statements, invoices, and receipts for reference and audit purposes.

3. **Use the Audit Log**

- QuickBooks Online's Audit Log tracks all changes, providing transparency and accountability.

4. Train Your Team

- Ensure employees or bookkeepers involved in the process understand the importance of accurate data entry and timely reconciliations.

5. Schedule Regular Reviews

- Set aside dedicated time each month to review and close the books, making it a routine part of your workflow.

7. Benefits of Closing the Books Regularly

Regularly closing the books offers several advantages:

- **Accurate Financial Records**: Ensures reports reflect the true financial position of your business.
- **Reduced Errors**: Catches mistakes or discrepancies before they become major issues.
- **Improved Tax Readiness**: Streamlines tax preparation, saving time and reducing stress.
- **Enhanced Decision-Making**: Provides reliable data for planning, budgeting, and forecasting.

Closing the books is a vital step in maintaining accurate financial records and preparing your business for tax season. By following a consistent process in QuickBooks Online, you can ensure your data is complete, secure, and ready for analysis or compliance requirements. This monthly routine not only reduces errors but also provides the insights you need to make informed decisions and achieve long-term success.

With your books closed and finances in order, you're well-equipped to handle tax season and confidently plan for the future. Keep this process as a cornerstone of your financial management to ensure a strong foundation for your business's growth.

BOOK 2

INTERMEDIATE TOOLS AND FEATURES

Welcome to **Book 2: Intermediate Tools and Features**, where we dive deeper into QuickBooks Online to explore its powerful tools and functionalities that take your financial management to the next level. Now that you've mastered the basics, it's time to optimize your workflow, enhance efficiency, and unlock features that help you save time and gain more control over your business operations.

This book focuses on intermediate-level tools designed to streamline your processes and improve your business performance. We'll start with **Chapter 5**, where you'll learn how to navigate and customize the QuickBooks Online interface, including shortcuts and interactive dashboard tips that make daily tasks faster and more intuitive.

In **Chapter 6**, we'll focus on sales and customer relations, guiding you through creating estimates and quotes, tracking payments, and handling refunds with ease. These features empower you to manage your sales pipeline effectively while maintaining strong customer relationships.

Chapter 7 is all about simplifying expense management. From organizing vendor profiles to automating bills and tracking mileage, you'll discover how QuickBooks Online minimizes manual effort while keeping your records accurate and organized.

Finally, **Chapter 8** introduces the world of app integrations. Learn how to connect QuickBooks with popular tools like PayPal, Shopify, and Square to enhance your workflows, manage inventory, and troubleshoot syncing issues effortlessly.

By the end of this book, you'll have a strong command of QuickBooks Online's intermediate tools, allowing you to run your business more efficiently and effectively. Let's dive in and unlock the full potential of these features!

CHAPTER 5

MASTERING THE NAVIGATION BAR

The navigation bar is the backbone of QuickBooks Online, giving you access to all the tools and features you need to manage your business finances. Understanding how to use and customize this essential component can save you time, simplify your workflow, and improve your overall efficiency.

In this chapter, we'll explore how to navigate and personalize the QuickBooks Online interface for maximum productivity. We'll start by **breaking down the key sections** of the navigation bar, such as Sales, Expenses, and Reports, helping you understand what each section offers and how to use it effectively. Whether you're managing invoices, tracking expenses, or generating financial reports, knowing where to find these tools is critical to keeping your operations running smoothly.

Next, we'll dive into **adding shortcuts for efficiency**, where you'll learn how to customize the navigation bar to match your workflow. By prioritizing the features and tools you use most, you can reduce clicks and access vital information faster, saving valuable time each day.

Finally, we'll share **interactive dashboard tips** to help you analyze your business performance directly from the QuickBooks Online dashboard. With insights into cash flow, sales trends, and overdue payments, you'll gain a real-time understanding of your financial health without having to generate detailed reports.

By mastering the navigation bar, you'll unlock the full potential of QuickBooks Online, making it easier to manage your business efficiently and stay on top of your finances. Let's get started!

Breaking Down Key Sections: Sales, Expenses, and More

The navigation bar in QuickBooks Online is your primary gateway to managing your business's finances. By understanding the purpose and functionality of its key sections, you can quickly access the tools you need and streamline your workflow. This guide provides an in-depth look at the most important sections of the navigation bar, including **Sales**, **Expenses**, **Banking**, **Reports**, and more, with practical tips on how to use them effectively.

1. The Sales Section: Managing Revenue Streams

The **Sales** section is where you manage your invoices, payments, customers, and sales performance. It's designed to help you track revenue and maintain strong customer relationships.

1.1. Invoices

- **Purpose**: Create, send, and track invoices.
- **How to Use**:
    1. Navigate to **Sales > Invoices**.
    2. Click **+ New Invoice** to create a new invoice.
    3. Track the status of existing invoices, such as Open, Paid, or Overdue.
- **Pro Tip**: Set up recurring invoices for regular clients to save time and ensure consistent billing.

1.2. Customers

- **Purpose**: Maintain customer profiles and transaction histories.
- **How to Use**:
    1. Go to **Sales > Customers**.
    2. Add new customers or edit existing profiles with contact details and preferences.
    3. View a customer's transaction history to track outstanding balances or recent activity.
- **Pro Tip**: Use notes to add specific details about customers, like preferred payment terms or special discounts.

1.3. Products and Services

- **Purpose**: Manage the items or services you sell.
- **How to Use**:
  1. Navigate to **Sales > Products and Services**.
  2. Add inventory items, non-inventory items, or services, including descriptions and pricing.
  3. Monitor inventory levels and set low-stock alerts.
- **Pro Tip**: Categorize products and services to simplify reporting and improve insights into sales trends.

2. The Expenses Section: Controlling Costs

The **Expenses** section is your go-to area for tracking and managing spending. Whether it's vendor payments, recurring bills, or mileage, this section helps you maintain control over your costs.

2.1. Vendors

- **Purpose**: Manage relationships with suppliers and contractors.
- **How to Use**:
  1. Go to **Expenses > Vendors**.
  2. Add vendor profiles with contact details and payment terms.
  3. Track all transactions with a specific vendor, including bills and payments.
- **Pro Tip**: Categorize vendors based on the type of expenses they provide for more granular reporting.

2.2. Bills and Payments

- **Purpose**: Record and manage outstanding bills and payments.
- **How to Use**:
  1. Navigate to **Expenses > Bills**.
  2. Create new bills for upcoming payments, specifying due dates and amounts.
  3. Mark bills as paid once transactions are completed.
- **Pro Tip**: Use the recurring bill feature for fixed monthly expenses like rent or subscriptions.

2.3. Mileage

- **Purpose**: Track business-related travel for tax deductions.
- **How to Use**:
    1. Go to **Expenses > Mileage**.
    2. Use the mobile app to track mileage automatically or enter trips manually.
    3. Categorize trips as business or personal.
- **Pro Tip**: Regularly review mileage reports to ensure you're capturing all deductible travel.

3. The Banking Section: Simplifying Financial Transactions

The **Banking** section allows you to connect your bank accounts and credit cards to QuickBooks Online, enabling automatic transaction imports and reconciliation.

3.1. Banking Overview

- **Purpose**: Access all linked accounts in one place.
- **How to Use**:
    1. Navigate to **Banking > Banking**.
    2. View real-time account balances and transactions.
    3. Match transactions to your QuickBooks records or categorize new ones.
- **Pro Tip**: Set up rules for recurring transactions, like categorizing all PayPal fees under "Bank Fees."

3.2. Reconciliation

- **Purpose**: Ensure your QuickBooks records match your bank statements.
- **How to Use**:
    1. Navigate to **Accounting > Reconcile**.
    2. Choose an account and compare your records with the statement.
    3. Adjust for discrepancies and finalize the reconciliation.
- **Pro Tip**: Reconcile accounts monthly to stay on top of your financial health and catch errors early.

4. The Reports Section: Gaining Insights

The **Reports** section is where you generate and analyze financial data, providing valuable insights into your business's performance.

4.1. Business Overview Reports

- **Purpose**: Assess your overall financial health.
- **Key Reports**:
- Profit & Loss: Tracks income and expenses to show net profit.
- Balance Sheet: Summarizes assets, liabilities, and equity.
- Cash Flow: Monitors money moving in and out of your business.
- **Pro Tip**: Customize reports to include specific timeframes, accounts, or categories.

4.2. Sales and Expense Reports

- **Purpose**: Analyze revenue and spending trends.
- **Key Reports**:
- Sales by Customer Summary: Identifies top clients.
- Expense by Vendor Summary: Highlights major suppliers and spending areas.
- **Pro Tip**: Use these reports to identify areas where you can cut costs or focus marketing efforts.

4.3. Accounts Receivable and Payable Reports

- **Purpose**: Track money owed to and by your business.
- **Key Reports**:
- A/R Aging Summary: Lists overdue invoices.
- A/P Aging Summary: Tracks outstanding bills.
- **Pro Tip**: Regularly review these reports to stay ahead of cash flow challenges.

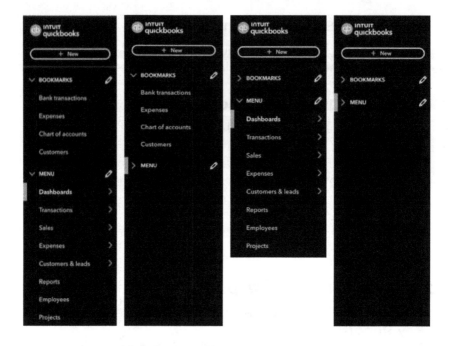

5. Additional Navigation Bar Sections

5.1. Apps

- **Purpose**: Integrate third-party tools to enhance QuickBooks functionality.
- **How to Use**:
  1. Navigate to **Apps** in the navigation bar.
  2. Browse recommended integrations like Shopify, PayPal, or CRM tools.
- **Pro Tip**: Choose apps that align with your business needs, such as inventory management or marketing automation.

5.2. Taxes

- **Purpose**: Manage sales tax, payroll tax, and other tax-related activities.
- **How to Use**:
  1. Go to **Taxes** in the navigation bar.
  2. Set up sales tax rates and monitor tax liabilities.
  3. Prepare and file tax returns directly from QuickBooks.

- **Pro Tip**: Use the tax summary report for a quick overview of your liabilities and deductions.

5.3. Projects

- **Purpose**: Track income, expenses, and profitability for individual projects.
- **How to Use**:
  1. Navigate to **Projects** in the navigation bar.
  2. Create a project and assign transactions like invoices or expenses.
  3. Generate project profitability reports.
- **Pro Tip**: Use projects to monitor job costs and ensure profitability on larger contracts.

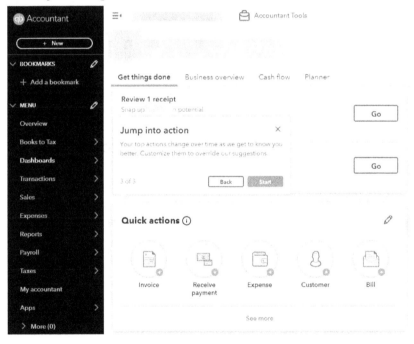

6. Customizing the Navigation Bar

The navigation bar can be customized to suit your workflow, ensuring you have quick access to the tools you use most.

6.1. Reordering Items

• Drag and drop menu items to reorganize the navigation bar.

6.2. Adding Shortcuts

• Use the **+ New** button to create shortcuts for common tasks like creating invoices or recording expenses.

6.3. Hiding Unused Sections

• Click the gear icon and deselect unused sections to declutter the interface.

Understanding and optimizing the navigation bar is essential for efficient financial management in QuickBooks Online. By mastering the **Sales**, **Expenses**, **Banking**, **Reports**, and other sections, you can streamline your workflow, save time, and gain deeper insights into your business. With the navigation bar customized to your needs, you're ready to tackle any financial task with confidence. Let's explore how adding shortcuts can further enhance your efficiency in the next section!

Adding Shortcuts for Efficiency: Customizing Your Workflow

Managing your business finances effectively requires tools that align with your unique workflow. QuickBooks Online offers a variety of ways to customize its interface, allowing you to create shortcuts and streamline repetitive tasks. By tailoring the platform to match your business needs, you can save time, reduce errors, and focus on what truly matters: growing your business.

This chapter explores how to add shortcuts, customize workflows, and utilize time-saving features in QuickBooks Online. Whether you're creating invoices, tracking expenses, or running reports, these strategies will help you navigate QuickBooks more efficiently.

1. Understanding Shortcuts in QuickBooks Online

Shortcuts in QuickBooks Online are customized links, buttons, or tools that provide direct access to frequently used features. These shortcuts reduce the number of clicks required to complete a task and make your workflow more efficient.

1.1. Types of Shortcuts

1. Navigation Bar Shortcuts

- Add or rearrange items in the navigation bar to prioritize your most-used sections.

2. + New Button Shortcuts

- Access commonly used tasks, such as creating invoices, recording expenses, or adding journal entries.

3. Custom Dashboard Widgets

- Customize the QuickBooks dashboard to display relevant widgets, such as income and expense summaries or overdue invoices.

4. Keyboard Shortcuts

- Use built-in keyboard commands to speed up navigation and data entry.

2. Adding and Rearranging Navigation Bar Shortcuts

The navigation bar in QuickBooks Online provides quick access to critical features. Customizing it allows you to prioritize the tools you use most frequently, reducing time spent searching for them.

2.1. Reordering Navigation Items

1. Access the Navigation Bar

- Navigate to the left-hand menu in QuickBooks Online.

2. Drag and Drop Items

- Click and hold a menu item, then drag it to your preferred position.

3. Save Your Changes

- The new order will be saved automatically, allowing you to access important features quickly.

2.2. Adding New Items

While QuickBooks Online doesn't allow you to add entirely new sections to the navigation bar, you can bookmark frequently accessed pages in your browser for quick access.

2.3. Hiding Unused Sections

1.   Access the Settings Menu

- Click the gear icon in the upper-right corner.

2.   Select Navigation Options

- Disable unused sections, such as "Mileage" or "Payroll," if they aren't relevant to your business.

3.   Focus on Essentials

- Streamline your navigation bar by keeping only the most critical items visible.

3. Customizing the + New Button for Quick Actions

The **+ New** button is a versatile tool in QuickBooks Online, providing shortcuts to create transactions, records, and reports. Customizing this menu ensures that your most frequently used tasks are always within reach.

3.1. Exploring the + New Button

- Access the **+ New** button in the upper-left corner of QuickBooks Online.
- The menu includes options for common actions like:
- **Customers**: Create invoices, sales receipts, or credit memos.
- **Vendors**: Record expenses, bills, or check payments.
- **Other**: Add journal entries, bank deposits, or transfers.

3.2. Prioritizing Common Tasks

1.   Identify Frequently Used Actions

- Determine which tasks you perform daily, such as creating invoices or recording expenses.

2. Bookmark Key Actions

- Save specific actions to your browser bookmarks for one-click access.

3. Group Tasks by Workflow

- For example, group customer-related tasks (invoices, payments) together for streamlined client management.

3.3. Automating Recurring Transactions

1. Create Recurring Templates

- Navigate to **Settings > Recurring Transactions** and set up templates for recurring tasks like monthly bills or subscriptions.

2. Enable Auto-Entry

- Configure templates to automatically create transactions, reducing manual data entry.

4. Using Custom Dashboard Widgets

The QuickBooks Online dashboard provides a high-level overview of your business's financial health. Customizing widgets allows you to prioritize the data and insights that matter most to your business.

4.1. Accessing the Dashboard

- From the QuickBooks Online homepage, you'll see widgets displaying cash flow, invoices, expenses, and more.

4.2. Customizing Widget Placement

1. Drag and Drop

- Click and hold a widget, then drag it to your preferred position.

2. Add or Remove Widgets

- Click the gear icon in the top-right corner of the dashboard.
- Enable or disable widgets based on your business needs.

4.3. Tailoring Widgets for Your Business

- **For Retailers**: Highlight sales and inventory metrics.

- **For Service Providers**: Focus on overdue invoices and cash flow.
- **For Freelancers**: Track expenses and profit margins.

4.4. Interactive Dashboard Tips

- Use the dashboard's real-time data to identify trends and anomalies quickly.
- Click on widgets to drill down into detailed reports or transaction histories.

5. Keyboard Shortcuts for Faster Navigation

QuickBooks Online includes several keyboard shortcuts to help you navigate the platform more efficiently.

5.1. Common Keyboard Shortcuts

1. **Ctrl + Alt +?**: Access the QuickBooks Online shortcuts menu.
2. **Ctrl + Alt + I**: Create an invoice.
3. **Ctrl + Alt + E**: Record an expense.
4. **Ctrl + Alt + R**: View a report.

5.2. Customizing Shortcuts

While QuickBooks Online doesn't allow custom keyboard shortcuts, you can create browser-based shortcuts for specific tasks.

6. Automating Workflows for Efficiency

In addition to shortcuts, QuickBooks Online offers automation features that reduce manual effort and streamline repetitive tasks.

6.1. Setting Up Rules for Transactions

1. **Navigate to Banking Rules**

- Go to **Banking > Rules**.

2. **Create a New Rule**

- Define criteria for recurring transactions, such as categorizing all payments to a specific vendor under "Office Supplies."

3. **Apply Rules Automatically**

- QuickBooks will categorize transactions that meet the rule's conditions, saving you time during reconciliation.

6.2. Automating Reports

1. **Customize Reports**

- Create a customized report and save it under **Reports > Custom Reports**.

2. **Schedule Reports**

- Set up automatic email delivery for key reports, like Profit & Loss or Balance Sheet, on a weekly or monthly basis.

7. Integrating with Third-Party Apps

Connecting QuickBooks Online to third-party apps enhances its functionality and further streamlines your workflow.

7.1. Popular App Integrations

- **PayPal**: Sync payments and expenses.
- **Shopify**: Manage inventory and track sales.
- **TSheets**: Automate time tracking and payroll.

7.2. Creating App-Based Shortcuts

- Use app integrations to perform tasks directly from third-party platforms, such as issuing invoices from Shopify.

8. Best Practices for Workflow Customization

1. **Regularly Review Your Shortcuts**

- Adjust shortcuts and navigation preferences as your business evolves.

2. **Focus on Efficiency**

- Identify bottlenecks in your workflow and use QuickBooks Online's customization options to address them.

3. **Train Your Team**

- Ensure all team members are familiar with the shortcuts and automation features you've implemented.

4. **Leverage Analytics**

- Use the dashboard and reports to identify areas where additional customization could save time or improve accuracy.

Adding shortcuts and customizing your workflow in QuickBooks Online is one of the easiest ways to improve efficiency and productivity. Whether you're reordering the navigation bar, creating custom dashboard widgets, or automating recurring tasks, these strategies allow you to tailor the platform to your business needs. By streamlining your processes, you'll save time, reduce errors, and focus more on growing your business. Now that you've optimized your workflow, let's explore how to analyze business performance using interactive dashboard tips in the next section!

Interactive Dashboard Tips: Analyzing Business Performance

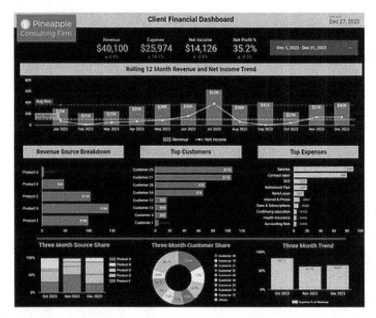

The QuickBooks Online dashboard is your command center for tracking your business's financial health. With real-time data and customizable widgets, the dashboard provides an at-a-glance overview of critical metrics such as cash flow, expenses, sales, and overdue invoices. Learning how to leverage the dashboard effectively can save time and help you make informed decisions to improve your business performance.

In this chapter, we'll explore how to maximize the QuickBooks Online dashboard by understanding its core features, customizing widgets, interpreting key metrics, and using the insights to analyze your business's performance. With these tips, you can transform your dashboard into a powerful tool for strategic decision-making.

1. Understanding the QuickBooks Online Dashboard

The QuickBooks Online dashboard is designed to provide a snapshot of your business's financial status. It includes several key widgets that update in real time, allowing you to monitor your finances without generating detailed reports.

1.1. Core Dashboard Widgets

1. **Cash Flow**
    - Tracks money coming in and going out of your business.
    - Includes forecasts based on pending invoices and bills.

2. **Profit and Loss Summary**
    - Displays your income, expenses, and net profit over a selected time period.

3. **Invoices**
    - Highlights overdue, open, and recently paid invoices.

4. **Expenses**
    - Categorizes spending by type (e.g., rent, utilities, marketing).

5. **Bank Accounts**
    - Shows real-time balances for connected bank and credit card accounts.

1.2. Benefits of Using the Dashboard

- **Real-Time Insights**: Instant updates keep you informed about your financial health.
- **Quick Access**: View essential metrics without running full reports.

- **Customizable Layout**: Tailor the dashboard to focus on the data that matters most to your business.

2. Customizing the Dashboard

Customizing your QuickBooks Online dashboard ensures it reflects the most relevant information for your business. By tailoring widgets and layout, you can streamline your workflow and prioritize key metrics.

2.1. Adding or Removing Widgets

1. **Click the Gear Icon**
- Located at the top right of the dashboard, the gear icon opens the customization menu.

2. **Enable or Disable Widgets**
- Check or uncheck widgets such as Invoices, Cash Flow, or Expenses.
- Focus on metrics that align with your business goals.

2.2. Rearranging Widgets

1. **Drag and Drop Widgets**
- Click on a widget's header and drag it to a new position.

2. **Prioritize Key Data**
- Place critical widgets like Cash Flow or Profit and Loss at the top for quick access.

2.3. Customizing Date Ranges

1. **Adjust Time Frames**
- Use the dropdown menus on widgets like Profit and Loss to select daily, weekly, monthly, or custom date ranges.

2. **Analyze Trends**
- Compare data over different periods to identify patterns in revenue, expenses, or cash flow.

3. Analyzing Key Metrics on the Dashboard

Each widget on the dashboard provides valuable insights into your business's performance. Understanding how to interpret these metrics is essential for making data-driven decisions.

3.1. Cash Flow Insights

1. **Monitor Incoming and Outgoing Funds**

- View how much money is coming in from customers and going out for expenses or vendor payments.

2. **Identify Cash Flow Gaps**

- Look for negative trends, such as more money going out than coming in, and take steps to address them.

3. **Use Cash Flow Forecasting**

- Leverage projected cash flow to plan for upcoming expenses or investments.

3.2. Profit and Loss Trends

1. **Evaluate Profitability**

- Compare income to expenses to see if your business is operating at a profit.

2. **Analyze Expense Categories**

- Identify which categories are consuming the most resources and look for ways to cut costs.

3. **Track Revenue Growth**

- Use year-over-year or month-over-month comparisons to assess growth trends.

3.3. Invoice Management

1. **Follow Up on Overdue Payments**

- Use the Invoices widget to identify overdue payments and send reminders.

2. **Monitor Open Invoices**

- Keep track of pending invoices to anticipate future cash flow.

3. **Analyze Payment Patterns**

- Identify customers who frequently pay late and consider adjusting terms or offering incentives for early payments.

3.4. Expense Monitoring

1. Categorize Spending

- Review the Expenses widget to ensure all transactions are categorized correctly for tax deductions.

2. Control Overspending

- Look for spikes in certain categories, such as travel or marketing, and adjust your budget accordingly.

3. Prepare for Tax Season

- Use categorized expenses to estimate deductions and streamline tax preparation.

4. Using the Dashboard for Strategic Decision-Making

The dashboard is not just for monitoring—it's a tool for making proactive decisions that can improve your business performance.

4.1. Planning for Growth

1. Identify Profitable Areas

- Use the Profit and Loss widget to see which products or services contribute most to your bottom line.

2. Allocate Resources

- Invest in high-performing areas and reduce spending on underperforming ones.

3. Set Financial Goals

- Use historical data to establish realistic revenue and expense targets.

4.2. Managing Cash Flow

1. Adjust Payment Terms

- Offer discounts for early payments or tighten payment deadlines to improve cash flow.

2. Delay Non-Essential Spending

- Postpone discretionary expenses during periods of low cash flow.

3. Build a Cash Reserve

- Use surplus funds to create a financial cushion for unexpected expenses.

4.3. Tracking Seasonal Trends

1. Compare Performance Periods

- Use date range filters to analyze seasonal fluctuations in revenue or expenses.

2. Prepare for Busy Seasons

- Increase inventory or staffing levels ahead of peak demand.

3. Plan for Slow Periods

- Reduce overhead or offer promotions to boost sales during slower months.

5. Advanced Tips for Maximizing the Dashboard

5.1. Integrating Third-Party Apps

- **Add Custom Widgets**: Use apps like Shopify or PayPal to display sales or transaction data directly on the dashboard.

5.2. Sharing Insights

- **Collaborate with Team Members**: Share dashboard data during meetings to align on financial goals and strategies.

5.3. Leveraging the Mobile App

- **Monitor On-the-Go**: Access the dashboard from your smartphone or tablet to stay updated while traveling.

5.4. Regularly Reviewing Metrics

- Schedule time each week or month to review dashboard data and adjust your strategies as needed.

6. Common Challenges and Solutions

6.1. Outdated Data

- **Solution**: Ensure all transactions are reconciled and bank feeds are up to date.

6.2. Irrelevant Widgets

- **Solution**: Remove widgets that don't add value and replace them with more useful ones.

6.3. Misinterpreting Metrics

- **Solution**: Consult with your accountant or financial advisor to validate your analysis and strategies.

The QuickBooks Online dashboard is a powerful tool for analyzing your business's financial performance. By customizing widgets, interpreting key metrics, and using insights to make strategic decisions, you can maintain a clear understanding of your financial health and identify opportunities for growth. With real-time updates and tailored layouts, your dashboard becomes more than just a summary—it's your financial command center.

Mastering the dashboard ensures you're always informed and prepared to navigate the complexities of running a business. Now that you've learned how to analyze business performance using the dashboard, let's explore sales and customer relations in the next chapter!

CHAPTER 6
SALES AND CUSTOMER RELATIONS

Sales and customer relationships are the lifeblood of any business, and managing them effectively is crucial for sustained success. QuickBooks Online provides a suite of tools to streamline your sales process, maintain strong customer relationships, and ensure smooth financial transactions. In this chapter, we'll explore how to leverage these features to optimize your sales and customer management workflow.

We'll begin by discussing **Drafting Estimates and Quotes**, a feature that simplifies creating professional, customizable estimates and quotes for your clients. You'll also learn how to convert these documents into invoices with just a few clicks, reducing administrative tasks and accelerating your sales process.

Next, we'll delve into **Tracking Payments**, a critical aspect of cash flow management. QuickBooks Online enables you to monitor overdue accounts, send payment reminders, and record payments efficiently, ensuring you're always up to date on your receivables.

Finally, we'll cover **Refunds and Credits**, which help you handle customer returns or adjustments with ease. QuickBooks Online's intuitive interface simplifies issuing refunds and applying credits, making the process transparent and professional.

By mastering these tools, you'll streamline your sales operations, improve customer satisfaction, and enhance your financial management. Whether you're drafting estimates, managing payments, or processing returns, QuickBooks Online ensures that every interaction with your customers is efficient and accurate. Let's dive in and explore how to strengthen your sales and customer relations!

Drafting Estimates and Quotes: Conversion to Invoices Made Easy

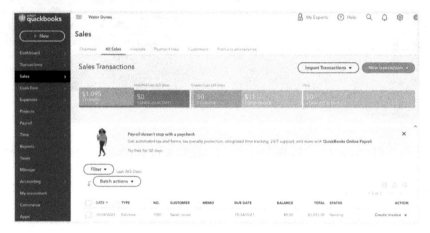

Creating accurate and professional estimates and quotes is an essential step in securing new business and maintaining strong client relationships. With QuickBooks Online, you can streamline this process by drafting, managing, and converting estimates and quotes into invoices effortlessly. This powerful feature ensures consistency across your sales process, saves time, and boosts your professionalism.

In this section, we'll explore the importance of estimates and quotes, guide you through creating and customizing them in QuickBooks Online, and explain how to seamlessly convert them into invoices.

1. The Importance of Estimates and Quotes

Estimates and quotes serve as the foundation for clear communication with your clients about the cost of products or services. They outline project scope, pricing, and terms, helping avoid misunderstandings and ensuring a smooth workflow.

1.1. Why They Matter

- **Transparency**: Provides clients with a clear understanding of pricing and deliverables.
- **Professionalism**: Enhances your brand image with detailed and accurate documentation.

- **Efficiency**: Establishes clear terms that reduce disputes or delays.

1.2. Key Differences

- **Estimate**: An approximate calculation of costs, often used when pricing may vary.
- **Quote**: A fixed offer that commits you to a specific price for a defined period.

Both can be created in QuickBooks Online and converted to invoices when the client agrees to the terms.

2. Creating Estimates and Quotes in QuickBooks Online

QuickBooks Online provides an intuitive interface for creating estimates and quotes tailored to your business needs.

2.1. Step-by-Step Guide to Creating an Estimate

1. **Navigate to the + New Button**

- On the QuickBooks dashboard, click the **+ New** button and select **Estimate** under the Customers section.

2. **Add Client Information**

- Choose an existing customer from the dropdown menu or create a new customer by entering their details.

3. **Specify the Estimate Details**

- Fill in key fields:
  - **Date**: Set the date the estimate is created.
  - **Expiration Date**: Specify how long the estimate is valid.

4. **List Products or Services**

- Add items or services, their descriptions, quantities, and rates. QuickBooks automatically calculates totals.

5. **Add Discounts or Taxes**

- Include any applicable discounts, sales tax, or additional charges.

6. **Customize the Layout**

- Use the **Customize** button to adjust branding elements like your logo, colors, and fonts.

7.   Save or Send

- Save the estimate as a draft for internal review or send it directly to the client via email.

2.2. Creating a Quote

Quotes in QuickBooks Online follow the same process as estimates but typically include more detailed terms and conditions to ensure pricing clarity.

3. Customizing Estimates and Quotes

QuickBooks Online allows you to tailor estimates and quotes to reflect your business's professionalism and brand identity.

3.1. Adding Personalization

- **Branding**: Upload your logo, select company colors, and use consistent fonts.
- **Language**: Customize terminology and add client-specific notes or terms.

3.2. Including Additional Details

- **Payment Terms**: Clearly define payment expectations (e.g., Net 30, Due on Receipt).
- **Deliverables**: Add a detailed breakdown of project scope or product descriptions.
- **Attachments**: Include relevant files, such as product photos or service agreements.

3.3. Saving Templates

Save customized formats as templates for future use, ensuring consistency across all estimates and quotes.

4. Managing Estimates and Quotes

QuickBooks Online simplifies the management of estimates and quotes, ensuring you can track their status and make necessary updates.

4.1. Viewing and Tracking

- Navigate to **Sales > All Sales** and filter by **Estimates** or **Quotes** to view all active documents.
- Check the status column for updates:
- **Pending**: Awaiting client approval.
- **Accepted**: Ready to convert to an invoice.
- **Closed**: Expired or no longer valid.

4.2. Editing or Updating

- Open the estimate or quote and click **Edit** to update pricing, quantities, or terms if needed.
- Notify the client of changes and resend the updated document.

4.3. Sending Reminders

- Use QuickBooks to send automated follow-up emails to clients who haven't responded to an estimate or quote.

5. Converting Estimates and Quotes to Invoices

One of the most powerful features of QuickBooks Online is the ability to convert estimates and quotes directly into invoices, streamlining your sales process and ensuring accuracy.

5.1. When to Convert

- Convert an estimate or quote to an invoice once the client has reviewed and approved the terms.
- Ensure all changes or additions have been finalized before conversion.

5.2. Steps to Convert

1. **Locate the Approved Document**

- Go to **Sales > All Sales** and find the estimate or quote marked as **Accepted**.

2. **Click on Convert to Invoice**

- Open the document and select **Create Invoice** from the actions menu.

3. **Review the Invoice**
- Confirm that all details, including pricing, taxes, and terms, are accurate.
- Add payment methods if applicable.

4. **Send the Invoice**
- Email the invoice to the client directly from QuickBooks or download it for printing.

5.3. Partial Invoicing
- For projects billed in phases, create partial invoices from an estimate by selecting specific line items or amounts to include.
- The remaining balance stays linked to the original estimate for future invoicing.

6. Automating the Process
Automation reduces manual effort and ensures consistency throughout the sales process.

6.1. Recurring Transactions
- For repeat customers or subscription services, create recurring templates that automatically generate estimates or invoices.

6.2. Reminders and Follow-Ups
- Set automated reminders for clients to approve estimates or quotes and to pay invoices on time.

6.3. Integrating with Other Tools
- Use apps like HubSpot or Salesforce to sync client data and streamline the sales workflow.

7. Best Practices for Estimates and Quotes
To maximize the effectiveness of your estimates and quotes, follow these best practices:

7.1. Provide Clear Details

- Include all relevant information to avoid misunderstandings, such as pricing breakdowns, timelines, and terms.

7.2. Maintain Consistency

- Use templates to ensure all documents follow the same format and branding.

7.3. Follow Up Promptly

- Contact clients who haven't responded within a reasonable time frame to keep projects moving.

7.4. Review Regularly

- Audit your estimates and quotes for accuracy and relevance, updating them as needed.

7.5. Track Performance

- Use QuickBooks reports to analyze conversion rates from estimates to invoices, identifying areas for improvement.

8. Benefits of Using QuickBooks Online for Estimates and Quotes

QuickBooks Online simplifies the entire process, offering several advantages:

- **Efficiency**: Reduce manual data entry and duplication.
- **Accuracy**: Ensure consistency between estimates, quotes, and invoices.
- **Professionalism**: Impress clients with detailed, branded documents.
- **Insights**: Track conversion rates and optimize your sales process.

Drafting estimates and quotes in QuickBooks Online is an essential step in managing your sales process. By creating professional, detailed documents and converting them seamlessly into invoices, you can enhance client relationships and improve your workflow. With the ability to customize, automate, and track these documents, QuickBooks Online empowers you to handle every step of the sales process efficiently and professionally.

Mastering estimates and quotes sets the foundation for smooth sales operations. Now that you've learned how to draft and manage them, let's move on to the next key element of sales and customer relations: tracking payments and managing overdue accounts!

Tracking Payments: Managing Overdue Accounts Effectively

Managing payments is critical for maintaining a healthy cash flow and ensuring your business operates smoothly. While most clients pay on time, overdue accounts are a common challenge for many businesses. QuickBooks Online offers powerful tools to help you track payments, manage overdue accounts, and encourage timely payments from customers. With a strategic approach and effective tools, you can reduce payment delays and improve your cash flow.

This chapter explores the importance of tracking payments, how to use QuickBooks Online to monitor and manage overdue accounts, and best practices to prevent late payments while maintaining strong customer relationships.

1. Why Tracking Payments Matters

Effective payment tracking is essential for several reasons:

1.1. Cash Flow Management

- Timely payments ensure you have the funds needed to cover expenses like payroll, inventory, and overhead costs.

1.2. Business Stability

- Overdue payments can strain your finances, delaying your ability to invest in growth or settle your own obligations.

1.3. Strong Customer Relationships

- Proactive payment management helps maintain positive relationships by addressing issues before they escalate.

By using QuickBooks Online to track payments, you can streamline your process and reduce the administrative burden.

2. Setting Up Payment Tracking in QuickBooks Online

QuickBooks Online makes it easy to track payments and monitor overdue accounts with intuitive tools and features.

2.1. Configuring Payment Terms

Setting clear payment terms is the first step to managing payments effectively.

1. **Go to Settings**
- Click the **Gear Icon** in the top-right corner and select **All Lists** > **Terms**.

2. **Create Payment Terms**
- Define terms such as **Net 30** (payment due 30 days after the invoice date) or **Due on Receipt**.

3. **Assign Terms to Customers**
- In the **Customers** tab, assign default payment terms to each customer for consistent tracking.

2.2. Enabling Payment Methods

Make it easy for customers to pay by enabling multiple payment methods.

1. Set Up QuickBooks Payments

•   Navigate to **Settings > Payments** and link payment options like credit cards, PayPal, or bank transfers.

2. Add Payment Links to Invoices

•   Include payment links on invoices for faster processing.

3. Monitoring Payments in QuickBooks Online

QuickBooks Online's interface allows you to view payment statuses, follow up on overdue accounts, and record payments efficiently.

3.1. Using the All Sales Tab

1. Navigate to Sales > All Sales

•   This section displays a list of all sales transactions, including invoices, payments, and credits.

2. Filter by Status

•   Use filters like **Overdue** or **Open Invoices** to identify outstanding payments quickly.

3. Track Payment Progress

•   Monitor the status of each invoice:
    □ **Paid**: Fully settled.
    □ **Partial**: Partially paid.
    □ **Overdue**: Past the due date with no payment.

3.2. Viewing Customer Balances

1. Go to Sales > Customers

•   View customer profiles to see outstanding balances and payment histories.

2. Generate Customer Statements

•   Create statements that summarize overdue invoices and send them to customers as reminders.

4. Managing Overdue Accounts

When payments become overdue, QuickBooks Online provides tools to address the issue efficiently and professionally.

4.1. Sending Payment Reminders

1. **Set Up Automatic Reminders**
- Navigate to **Settings > Automation** and enable payment reminders. Customize the timing, such as 3 days before or 7 days after the due date.

2. **Send Manual Reminders**
- Open an overdue invoice and select **Send Reminder** to email the customer directly.

3. **Craft Professional Messages**
- Use polite but firm language in reminders:
  - Example: "Hello [Customer Name], this is a friendly reminder that Invoice #1234, due on [Due Date], is currently overdue. Please let us know if you have any questions or need assistance."

4.2. Applying Late Fees

1. **Enable Late Fees**
- Go to **Settings > All Lists > Terms** and configure late fees, such as a percentage of the invoice total or a flat fee.

2. **Add Late Fees to Invoices**
- Late fees are automatically applied to overdue invoices based on the terms you've set.

4.3. Offering Payment Plans

1. **Negotiate Installments**
- Work with customers facing financial difficulties to establish a payment plan.

2. **Track Installments**
- Record partial payments in QuickBooks Online and monitor remaining balances.

5. Recording Payments

Recording payments accurately ensures your books stay balanced and up-to-date.

5.1. Recording Full Payments

1. **Open the Invoice**
- Go to **Sales > All Sales** and select the invoice being paid.

2. **Record Payment**
- Click **Receive Payment**, select the payment method, and enter the amount received.

3. **Save and Close**
- The invoice status updates to **Paid** automatically.

5.2. Recording Partial Payments

1. **Enter Partial Amount**
- In the **Receive Payment** window, input the amount received, leaving the remaining balance open.

2. **Track Remaining Balance**
- The invoice remains in the **Open** status until fully paid.

5.3. Handling Overpayments

1. **Record Overpayment**
- Enter the full payment amount, even if it exceeds the invoice total.

2. **Apply Credit**
- Issue a credit memo for the overpaid amount or apply it to future invoices.

6. Best Practices for Preventing Overdue Payments

Preventing overdue payments is always better than managing them. Implement these strategies to encourage timely payments:

6.1. Set Clear Expectations

- Include payment terms on all invoices and ensure customers understand them.

6.2. Offer Early Payment Discounts

- Incentivize timely payments with small discounts for customers who pay early, such as 2% off if paid within 10 days.

6.3. Simplify Payment Methods

- Offer multiple payment options, including credit cards, ACH transfers, and online payment portals.

6.4. Build Strong Relationships

- Maintain regular communication with clients and address disputes or concerns promptly to avoid delays.

7. Using Reports to Analyze Payment Trends

QuickBooks Online provides robust reporting tools to analyze payment trends and identify areas for improvement.

7.1. Accounts Receivable Aging Summary

- View overdue invoices by age group (e.g., 1-30 days, 31-60 days) to prioritize follow-ups.

7.2. Customer Payment History

- Analyze payment trends for individual customers to identify chronic late payers.

7.3. Cash Flow Reports

- Monitor incoming payments and assess how delays impact your cash flow.

8. Managing Disputes

Occasionally, customers may dispute an invoice or delay payment due to misunderstandings or financial difficulties.

8.1. Addressing Disputes

1.   Communicate Clearly

- Discuss the issue with the customer and provide documentation supporting the invoice.

2.   Offer Solutions

- Negotiate adjustments, such as discounts or payment plans, to resolve the issue.

8.2. Escalating When Necessary

- If the customer remains unresponsive, consider sending a formal demand letter or engaging a collection agency as a last resort.

9. Benefits of Effective Payment Tracking

By using QuickBooks Online to track payments and manage overdue accounts, you can:

- **Maintain Healthy Cash Flow**: Timely payments ensure you have funds to meet obligations and invest in growth.
- **Save Time**: Automated reminders and tracking reduce manual effort.
- **Enhance Customer Relationships**: Professional communication builds trust and encourages repeat business.

Tracking payments and managing overdue accounts effectively is essential for running a financially stable business. With QuickBooks Online's robust tools, you can monitor payments, follow up on overdue accounts, and maintain accurate records with ease. By implementing best practices, automating reminders, and analyzing payment trends, you'll improve your cash flow and strengthen customer relationships.

Now that you've mastered payment tracking, let's move on to the next critical aspect of sales and customer relations: handling refunds and credits efficiently.

Refunds and Credits: Simplifying Customer Returns

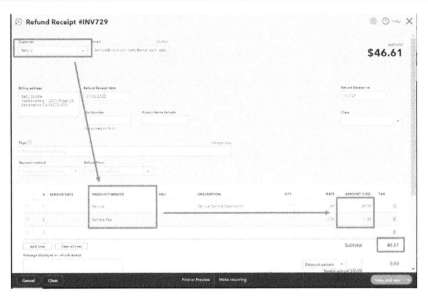

Handling refunds and credits is a critical part of maintaining excellent customer service and managing financial records accurately. While returns and adjustments may feel like a setback, they are an essential component of customer satisfaction and trust. QuickBooks Online simplifies this process, allowing you to issue refunds, apply credits, and maintain accurate records with ease.

In this chapter, we'll explore the importance of managing refunds and credits, how to handle them effectively in QuickBooks Online, and best practices for streamlining your workflow while maintaining customer relationships.

1. The Importance of Managing Refunds and Credits

Refunds and credits serve as a remedy when a customer isn't satisfied with a product or service. When handled professionally and efficiently, they can strengthen your relationship with the customer and protect your reputation.

1.1. Building Customer Trust

- Providing timely refunds or credits shows customers that you value their business and are committed to resolving issues fairly.

1.2. Maintaining Financial Accuracy

- Properly recorded refunds and credits ensure that your financial records and reports remain accurate, avoiding discrepancies during tax preparation or audits.

1.3. Complying with Policies and Regulations

- Issuing refunds and credits according to your business policies ensures compliance with consumer protection laws and regulations.

2. Types of Refunds and Credits

QuickBooks Online supports various types of refunds and credits to address different customer needs:

2.1. Full Refunds

- Issued when the customer returns a product or cancels a service in full.
- Example: A customer returns a defective product for a complete refund.

2.2. Partial Refunds

- Issued when only part of the product or service is returned or when a discount is provided as compensation.
- Example: A customer keeps the product but receives a partial refund due to minor damage.

2.3. Credits

- Issued to apply a credit amount to the customer's account for future purchases.
- Example: A customer receives a credit to use against their next invoice due to a delayed delivery.

2.4. Exchanges

- Processed when a product is returned but replaced with another product of equal or similar value.

3. Setting Up Refund and Credit Policies

Clear refund and credit policies make it easier to handle returns consistently and professionally.

3.1. Define Policies

- Clearly state the terms and conditions for refunds, credits, and exchanges in your sales agreements or invoices.
- Example: "Refunds accepted within 30 days of purchase with proof of receipt."

3.2. Communicate with Customers

- Ensure customers are aware of your policies at the time of purchase.
- Include the policies on invoices, estimates, or your website.

3.3. Train Your Team

- Train employees on how to handle refund and credit requests to ensure consistency and professionalism.

4. Processing Refunds in QuickBooks Online

QuickBooks Online makes it easy to issue and record refunds, ensuring your financial records stay accurate.

4.1. Issuing a Refund

1. **Navigate to the + New Button**

- On the dashboard, click **+ New** and select **Refund Receipt** under the Customers section.

2. **Enter Customer Information**

- Select the customer receiving the refund from the dropdown menu.

3. **Add Refunded Items**

- Enter the items or services being refunded, including quantities, rates, and amounts.

4. **Specify Payment Details**

- Indicate the refund method (e.g., cash, check, credit card) and ensure the correct bank or payment account is selected.

5. **Save and Close**

- The refund receipt updates your records and reduces income appropriately.

4.2. Refunding a Credit Card Payment

1. **Access the Payments Tab**

- Go to **Sales > Payments** and locate the original transaction.

2. **Initiate the Refund**

- Click **Refund** and follow the prompts to process the return to the customer's credit card.

5. Applying Credits in QuickBooks Online

Credits are an excellent alternative to refunds, especially when customers prefer to use the amount toward future purchases.

5.1. Creating a Credit Memo

1. **Navigate to the + New Button**

- Click **+ New** and select **Credit Memo** under the Customers section.

2. **Enter Customer Details**

- Choose the customer who will receive the credit.

3. **Add Credit Information**

- Specify the items, amounts, or services being credited, ensuring details align with the customer's expectations.

4. **Save and Close**

- The credit memo is now available to apply to future invoices.

5.2. Applying a Credit Memo to an Invoice

1. **Open the Customer's Profile**

- Go to **Sales > Customers** and select the relevant customer.

2. **Locate the Invoice**

- Find the open invoice to which you want to apply the credit.

3. **Apply the Credit**

- Open the invoice, click **Receive Payment**, and select the available credit to reduce the balance.

4. **Save and Close**

- The credit is deducted, and the invoice is updated.

6. Handling Exchanges

QuickBooks Online doesn't have a direct "exchange" feature, but you can process exchanges by combining refunds and new sales.

1. **Issue a Refund**

- Follow the steps above to refund the returned item.

2. **Create a New Sale**

- Generate a new invoice or sales receipt for the replacement item.

3. **Link Transactions**

- Include a note in both transactions to reference the exchange for record-keeping.

7. Recording Refunds and Credits for Accuracy

Properly recording refunds and credits ensures your financial records are accurate, which is essential for reporting and analysis.

7.1. Review Refund Reports

- Use the **Refunds Summary Report** in QuickBooks Online to monitor the volume and frequency of refunds.
- Identify patterns or recurring issues, such as defective products or service gaps.

7.2. Track Credit Usage

- Generate reports to view how credits are being applied and ensure all outstanding credits are used appropriately.

8. Best Practices for Managing Refunds and Credits

8.1. Act Promptly

- Process refunds and credits quickly to maintain customer satisfaction.

8.2. Document Everything

- Keep detailed records of all refund and credit transactions, including reasons for the return and customer communication.

8.3. Analyze Trends

- Use data from refunds and credits to identify issues with specific products, services, or policies.

8.4. Balance Refund Policies

- Be generous enough to build trust but firm enough to protect your business from abuse.

8.5. Offer Alternatives

- When possible, offer credits or exchanges instead of full refunds to retain revenue and customer loyalty.

9. Benefits of Efficient Refund and Credit Management

Handling refunds and credits effectively provides several advantages:

- **Improved Customer Retention**: Satisfied customers are more likely to return, even after a return or refund.
- **Enhanced Reputation**: Positive experiences with returns build trust and encourage word-of-mouth referrals.
- **Accurate Financial Records**: Properly recorded refunds and credits ensure your reports reflect the true state of your finances.
- **Better Business Insights**: Analyzing return data helps you identify areas for improvement in products or services.

Refunds and credits are a natural part of doing business, but they don't have to be a burden. With QuickBooks Online's intuitive tools and features, you can process returns, issue credits, and maintain accurate financial records effortlessly. By managing refunds and credits effectively, you'll enhance customer satisfaction, protect your business's reputation, and gain valuable insights into areas for improvement.

By implementing these strategies, you can simplify the process of handling refunds and credits while maintaining trust and loyalty with your customers. With this foundation, let's explore the next chapter and continue optimizing your sales and customer relations workflow!

CHAPTER 7
EXPENSE MANAGEMENT SIMPLIFIED

Managing expenses is a cornerstone of financial success for any business. Proper expense management ensures that your cash flow remains stable, your records are accurate, and your business operates efficiently. QuickBooks Online offers a range of tools to help you simplify and streamline this crucial aspect of your operations.

In this chapter, we'll explore how to make expense management easier and more effective. First, we'll look at **Vendor Management**, a feature that helps you organize vendor profiles, track transactions, and build stronger relationships with suppliers. By keeping vendor information up-to-date and easily accessible, you can streamline payments and maintain good standing with your partners.

Next, we'll discuss **Automating Bills and Recurring Payments**, a powerful way to reduce manual effort and ensure you never miss a payment. Automation not only saves time but also reduces errors and late fees, helping you focus on strategic business activities rather than administrative tasks.

Finally, we'll cover **Mileage Tracking**, a tool designed to help you log business-related travel expenses accurately. Whether you're driving to meet clients or making deliveries, QuickBooks Online's mileage tracking feature simplifies expense reporting and ensures you maximize tax deductions.

By the end of this chapter, you'll have a solid understanding of how to use QuickBooks Online's tools to manage expenses efficiently, improve record-keeping, and save time. Let's dive in and explore these features in detail!

Vendor Management: Organizing Profiles for Easier Transactions

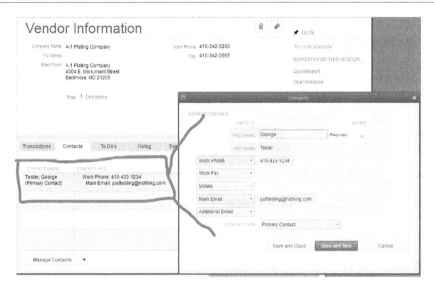

Effective vendor management is essential for maintaining smooth operations and ensuring timely payments to suppliers and service providers. In QuickBooks Online, vendor management tools allow you to create, organize, and maintain detailed vendor profiles, track transactions, and streamline your expense workflows. By mastering vendor management, you can save time, reduce errors, and maintain strong relationships with your suppliers.

This chapter will guide you through the process of setting up and organizing vendor profiles in QuickBooks Online, tracking transactions efficiently, and using these tools to make vendor relationships a seamless part of your financial operations.

1. Why Vendor Management Matters

Vendor management goes beyond simply paying bills. It's about fostering strong relationships with suppliers, organizing critical business data, and streamlining financial processes.

1.1. Importance of Vendor Management

- **Efficiency**: Centralized vendor profiles ensure you have quick access to contact details, payment terms, and transaction history.
- **Accuracy**: Organized vendor records help you categorize expenses correctly, reducing errors in financial reports.
- **Relationships**: Clear and timely communication with vendors fosters trust and collaboration.

1.2. Key Benefits

- Saves time during payment processing.
- Simplifies tax preparation by ensuring expenses are categorized correctly.
- Provides insights into spending patterns, enabling cost-saving decisions.

2. Setting Up Vendor Profiles

Creating detailed vendor profiles in QuickBooks Online is the first step to effective vendor management.

2.1. Adding a New Vendor

1. **Navigate to Vendors**
- Go to **Expenses > Vendors** in the QuickBooks Online navigation menu.

2. **Click New Vendor**
- Select the **New Vendor** button to open the vendor creation form.

3. **Enter Vendor Details**
- Include the following:
  - Name or Business Name.
  - Contact Information (phone, email, and address).
  - Payment Terms (e.g., Net 30, Net 15).
  - Tax ID, if applicable.

4. **Add Additional Notes**
- Record specific details such as preferred payment methods or key contacts at the vendor's company.

5. Save
- Once completed, click **Save** to create the profile.

2.2. Organizing Vendor Profiles

1. Group Vendors by Category
- Categorize vendors based on the type of service or product they provide, such as "Office Supplies," "Utilities," or "Professional Services."

2. Add Custom Fields
- Use custom fields to track unique information, such as contract renewal dates or discount terms.

3. Archive Inactive Vendors
- Mark inactive vendors as archived to keep your list organized without losing historical data.

3. Tracking Vendor Transactions

QuickBooks Online provides tools to track vendor-related transactions, ensuring your records are accurate and up-to-date.

3.1. Viewing Vendor Activity

1. Access Vendor Profiles
- Go to **Expenses > Vendors** and click on a vendor's name to open their profile.

2. Transaction List
- View a complete list of transactions, including bills, payments, and purchase orders.

3. Generate Reports
- Use reports such as "Vendor Balance Detail" to analyze unpaid balances and past transactions.

3.2. Recording Bills and Payments

1. Create a Bill
- Click **+ New** and select **Bill** under the Vendors section.

- Enter details such as the vendor name, invoice number, payment terms, and due date.

2. Record a Payment

- Once a bill is paid, click **+ New** and select **Pay Bills.**
- Choose the bill to pay, select the payment method, and confirm the transaction.

3.3. Managing Credits

- Apply vendor credits directly to bills by selecting the credit from the available balance during payment processing.

4. Streamlining Vendor Payments

QuickBooks Online simplifies the payment process, ensuring that bills are paid on time and accurately.

4.1. Automating Payments

1. Set Up Recurring Bills

- For recurring expenses, such as rent or utilities, create recurring transactions in **Settings > Recurring Transactions** to automate bill entries.

2. Schedule Payments

- Use connected bank accounts to schedule payments directly from QuickBooks Online.

4.2. Tracking Payment Status

- Use the **Expenses > Vendors** tab to view the status of bills:
- **Open**: Unpaid bills.
- **Overdue**: Bills past their due date.
- **Paid**: Completed transactions.

5. Analyzing Vendor Data

Understanding your spending patterns can help you optimize costs and identify opportunities for better vendor relationships.

5.1. Generating Vendor Reports

1. Expense by Vendor Summary

- Navigate to **Reports** and select the "Expense by Vendor Summary" report to see total spending per vendor.

2. Unpaid Bills Detail

- Use this report to identify outstanding balances and prioritize payments.

5.2. Monitoring Vendor Performance

- Track metrics such as delivery timelines, pricing consistency, and service quality to evaluate vendor performance.

6. Best Practices for Vendor Management

Efficient vendor management requires a proactive approach. Here are some best practices to keep in mind:

6.1. Maintain Up-to-Date Profiles

- Regularly review and update vendor profiles to ensure accuracy. Include new contact details, tax information, and payment terms as needed.

6.2. Categorize Expenses

- Use detailed categories to simplify tax preparation and gain insights into spending patterns.

6.3. Communicate Effectively

- Notify vendors promptly about issues such as invoice discrepancies or payment delays.

6.4. Negotiate Terms

- Leverage data from vendor reports to negotiate better payment terms, discounts, or bulk pricing.

6.5. Archive Inactive Vendors

- Periodically archive vendors you no longer work with to keep your records organized.

7. Leveraging Vendor Management for Cost Savings

By analyzing vendor data and optimizing your processes, you can uncover opportunities to reduce expenses:

1. **Identify High-Cost Vendors**
- Use vendor reports to pinpoint areas where costs can be reduced.

2. **Consolidate Purchases**
- Reduce expenses by consolidating purchases with a single vendor to qualify for bulk discounts.

3. **Negotiate Payment Terms**
- Extend payment terms with reliable vendors to improve cash flow.

4. **Evaluate Alternatives**
- Periodically review vendor performance and consider switching to more cost-effective options if needed.

8. Common Challenges and Solutions

While QuickBooks Online makes vendor management straightforward, challenges may arise:

8.1. Missing Information

- **Solution**: Use reminders in QuickBooks to prompt follow-ups for missing invoices or details.

8.2. Overdue Payments

- **Solution**: Monitor the **Unpaid Bills Report** regularly to avoid missing payment deadlines.

8.3. Duplicate Vendors

- **Solution**: Merge duplicate vendor profiles using the **Merge Vendors** tool in QuickBooks.

9. Benefits of Effective Vendor Management

A streamlined vendor management system offers numerous benefits:

- **Time Savings**: Organized profiles and automated processes reduce administrative tasks.
- **Improved Accuracy**: Ensures expenses are categorized correctly, leading to more accurate financial reporting.
- **Better Relationships**: Prompt and professional interactions with vendors build trust and foster collaboration.
- **Cost Optimization**: Data insights enable smarter spending decisions.

Effective vendor management is essential for keeping your business running smoothly and your finances in order. QuickBooks Online provides the tools to create and maintain detailed vendor profiles, track transactions, and streamline payments, all while fostering strong supplier relationships. By implementing the strategies and best practices discussed in this chapter, you'll not only simplify your expense workflows but also unlock opportunities to save time, reduce costs, and improve your overall financial management.

With vendor management mastered, you're well on your way to simplifying expense tracking and improving operational efficiency. Next, we'll explore how automating bills and recurring payments can take your expense management to the next level!

Automating Bills and Recurring Payments: Reducing Manual Effort

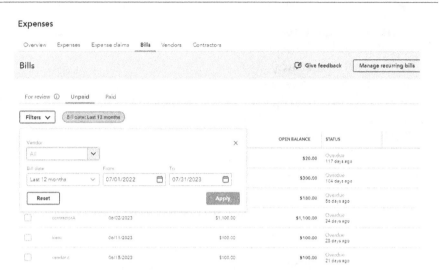

Managing bills and payments is a time-consuming but crucial part of running a business. Delays, errors, and missed deadlines can disrupt cash flow, damage vendor relationships, and incur penalties. Automating bills and recurring payments in Quick-Books Online can eliminate these issues, save time, and allow you to focus on growing your business. By leveraging automation, you can streamline processes, ensure accuracy, and maintain a consistent payment schedule.

This chapter delves into the benefits of automating bills and recurring payments, step-by-step instructions for setting up automation in QuickBooks Online, and best practices to maximize efficiency while maintaining control over your finances.

1. Why Automate Bills and Recurring Payments?

Automation offers numerous advantages for businesses looking to simplify their financial processes.

1.1. Time Savings

- Eliminates repetitive manual tasks, freeing up time for strategic activities.
- Reduces the need for constant monitoring and intervention.

1.2. Accuracy

- Minimizes the risk of human errors, such as entering incorrect amounts or missing due dates.
- Ensures consistent categorization of expenses for accurate financial records.

1.3. Cash Flow Management

- Keeps payment schedules predictable, helping you maintain stable cash flow.
- Avoids late fees and penalties by ensuring timely payments.

1.4. Strengthened Vendor Relationships

- Consistent and timely payments build trust with suppliers and improve long-term partnerships.

2. Setting Up Bill Automation in QuickBooks Online

QuickBooks Online provides an intuitive way to automate your bill entries, ensuring that recurring expenses are recorded and processed on time.

2.1. Creating a New Bill

1. **Navigate to the + New Button**

- From the dashboard, click **+ New** and select **Bill** under the Vendors section.

2. **Enter Vendor Details**

- Choose the vendor from your list or add a new vendor.
- Include relevant details like the invoice number, bill date, and payment terms.

3. **Itemize Expenses**

- Add line items to describe the goods or services provided, including quantities, rates, and amounts.

4. **Assign Categories**

- Categorize the expense appropriately (e.g., utilities, rent, office supplies).

5. **Save the Bill**

- Click **Save and Close** to record the bill in your accounts.

2.2. Automating Bills

1. **Set Up Recurring Bills**
- Navigate to **Settings > Recurring Transactions**.
- Click **New Transaction** and select **Bill** as the transaction type.

2. **Configure Recurrence**
- Choose the frequency (e.g., weekly, monthly, quarterly).
- Set start and end dates or make the recurrence indefinite.

3. **Customize Fields**
- Fill in details like vendor name, payment amount, and expense category.
- Add notes or memos for internal tracking.

4. **Save the Recurring Template**
- Once set up, QuickBooks Online will automatically generate the bill based on your chosen schedule.

3. Automating Recurring Payments

In addition to automating bill entries, QuickBooks Online allows you to automate payments to streamline the entire process.

3.1. Setting Up Bank Integration

1. **Link Your Bank Account**
- Navigate to **Banking > Link Account** and connect your bank or credit card accounts to QuickBooks Online.

2. **Enable Online Payments**
- Activate online payment options for bills, allowing QuickBooks to process payments directly through your linked accounts.

3.2. Scheduling Payments

1. **Go to Pay Bills**
- Click **+ New > Pay Bills** and select the bills you want to pay.

2. **Select Payment Method**

- Choose your preferred payment method (e.g., ACH transfer, credit card).

3. **Schedule Payment Date**

- Set the payment date, ensuring it aligns with your cash flow needs.

4. **Enable Automatic Payments**

- For recurring bills, enable the auto-pay feature to process payments without manual intervention.

3.3. Using Third-Party Payment Processors

- Integrate with tools like Bill.com or PayPal to automate payments for vendors that prefer external platforms.

4. Monitoring Automated Transactions

Automation reduces manual effort, but regular monitoring is essential to ensure accuracy and control.

4.1. Reviewing Scheduled Transactions

1. **Recurring Transactions List**

- Navigate to **Settings > Recurring Transactions** to view all automated entries.

2. **Edit or Pause Recurrences**

- Update amounts, dates, or frequencies as needed, or pause a recurrence temporarily.

4.2. Reconciling Accounts

- Reconcile your bank accounts monthly to verify that all automated payments match your QuickBooks records.

4.3. Generating Reports

- Use reports like **Recurring Transaction List** or **Expense by Vendor Summary** to review automated payments and identify trends.

5. Best Practices for Automating Bills and Payments

Automation is powerful, but it requires thoughtful implementation to avoid errors or oversight.

5.1. Start with Fixed Expenses

- Automate bills with consistent amounts and schedules, such as rent, utilities, or subscriptions.

5.2. Review Regularly

- Periodically review automated transactions to ensure they remain accurate and relevant.

5.3. Keep Sufficient Funds

- Ensure your bank account has adequate funds to cover automated payments and avoid overdraft fees.

5.4. Maintain Vendor Communication

- Inform vendors about your automated payment setup to ensure smooth processing and address any concerns.

5.5. Use Alerts

- Enable email or dashboard alerts for upcoming payments or changes to recurring transactions.

6. Troubleshooting Common Automation Issues

While automation simplifies workflows, occasional issues may arise. Here's how to address them:

6.1. Payment Errors

- **Issue**: Payments fail due to insufficient funds or incorrect account details.
- **Solution**: Double-check bank account information and maintain a buffer in your account.

6.2. Incorrect Amounts

- **Issue**: Changes in vendor pricing are not reflected in automated bills.
- **Solution**: Update recurring templates immediately when pricing changes occur.

6.3. Duplicate Transactions

- **Issue**: Automated entries are duplicated, leading to overpayments.
- **Solution**: Review recurring transactions and cross-check with vendor invoices.

7. Benefits of Automating Bills and Payments

Automation in QuickBooks Online offers transformative benefits for your business:

7.1. Efficiency

- Reduces the administrative burden of manual data entry and payment processing.

7.2. Accuracy

- Ensures consistent categorization of expenses, minimizing errors in financial records.

7.3. Timeliness

- Eliminates the risk of late payments, avoiding penalties and maintaining vendor trust.

7.4. Insights

- Provides detailed reporting on automated transactions, enabling better financial planning.

8. Advanced Automation Tips

To maximize the benefits of automation, consider these advanced tips:

8.1. Integrate with Accounting Tools

- Connect QuickBooks Online with third-party tools like Hub-Spot or Salesforce for seamless data flow.

8.2. Leverage Bulk Automation

- Use bulk upload features to automate large volumes of re-curring bills at once.

8.3. Schedule Custom Alerts

- Set reminders for when recurring transactions need review or renewal.

Automating bills and recurring payments in QuickBooks Online is a game-changer for businesses seeking efficiency and accuracy in their financial processes. By eliminating repetitive tasks, reducing errors, and ensuring timely payments, automation allows you to focus on strategic growth and operational excellence. With the tools and best practices outlined in this chapter, you can implement a seamless automation system that saves time, strengthens vendor relationships, and keeps your finances on track.

Now that you've streamlined your bill and payment workflows, let's explore another essential aspect of expense management: tracking mileage accurately to optimize your financial records and maximize tax deductions.

Mileage Tracking: Tools for Accurate Expense Reports

Mileage tracking is an essential aspect of managing business travel expenses, especially for small business owners, freelancers, and employees who use their vehicles for work-related purposes. Accurately tracking your mileage not only ensures your expense reports are precise but also helps you maximize tax deductions and reimbursements. QuickBooks Online provides powerful tools for seamless mileage tracking, offering accuracy, efficiency, and compliance with tax regulations.

In this chapter, we'll explore the benefits of mileage tracking, guide you through using QuickBooks Online's mileage features, and share best practices for maintaining detailed, compliant mileage records.

1. Why Accurate Mileage Tracking Matters

Tracking mileage accurately isn't just a good habit; it's a financial and legal necessity.

1.1. Tax Deductions

The IRS allows businesses to deduct mileage for eligible work-related trips. For 2024, the standard mileage rate is **65.5 cents per mile** (subject to change annually). Accurate tracking ensures you claim every mile you're entitled to.

1.2. Employee Reimbursements

Employers reimbursing employees for business-related vehicle use rely on accurate mileage logs to calculate fair reimbursements.

1.3. Audit Compliance

Detailed records ensure compliance with IRS requirements in case of an audit. The IRS mandates that mileage logs include the date, destination, purpose, and number of miles traveled.

1.4. Financial Clarity

Mileage tracking provides insights into your travel-related expenses, helping you budget more effectively and manage costs.

2. QuickBooks Online Mileage Tracking Features

QuickBooks Online simplifies mileage tracking with a user-friendly interface and automation tools designed to minimize manual effort.

2.1. Automatic Mileage Tracking

QuickBooks Online's mobile app includes a built-in mileage tracker that uses GPS to automatically record trips.

1.   **Enable Mileage Tracking**
- Open the QuickBooks Online mobile app.
- Navigate to **Mileage** in the menu and enable location tracking.

2.   **Start Driving**

- The app automatically detects when you're driving and logs the trip in real-time.

3. Review Trips

- After completing a trip, review the recorded details and categorize it as **Business** or **Personal**.

2.2. Manual Mileage Entry

For trips not automatically recorded, you can manually log mileage.

1. Navigate to the Mileage Tab

- Open the **Mileage** section in QuickBooks Online or the mobile app.

2. Add a New Trip

- Enter the trip's date, starting point, destination, purpose, and total miles traveled.

3. Save the Entry

- QuickBooks calculates the reimbursement or deduction amount based on the mileage rate.

2.3. Mileage Reports

QuickBooks Online generates detailed mileage reports that summarize your trips, total miles, and reimbursement or deduction values.

1. Access Reports

- Navigate to the **Reports** section and select a mileage report.

2. Customize Report Parameters

- Filter by date range, trip type (business or personal), or purpose.

3. Export and Share

- Export the report as a PDF or Excel file for tax filing or reimbursement purposes.

3. Setting Up Mileage Tracking

Setting up mileage tracking in QuickBooks Online ensures you capture accurate records from day one.

3.1. Configure Mileage Preferences

1.   Access Settings

- Go to **Settings > Mileage Settings**.

2.   Set Default Rates

- Enter the applicable mileage rate (e.g., IRS rate for business miles or your company's reimbursement rate).

3.   Enable Notifications

- Turn on alerts for unreviewed trips to avoid missing entries.

3.2. Link Personal and Business Vehicles

QuickBooks Online allows you to manage multiple vehicles, distinguishing between personal and business use.

1.   Add Vehicle Details

- Enter the make, model, and year of your vehicles in the **Mileage Settings** section.

2.   Track Usage by Vehicle

- Assign trips to specific vehicles for detailed reporting.

4. Categorizing Mileage

Correctly categorizing mileage is essential for accurate expense reporting and tax deductions.

4.1. Business Mileage

Eligible business trips include:

- Traveling to meet clients or suppliers.
- Attending off-site business meetings or conferences.
- Delivering goods or providing services to customers.

4.2. Personal Mileage

Trips unrelated to business, such as commuting from home to a regular workplace, are classified as personal mileage and are not deductible.

4.3. Mixed-Use Trips

For trips that include both business and personal purposes, only the business portion of the trip is deductible. QuickBooks allows you to split trips into multiple entries.

5. Maximizing Tax Deductions with Mileage Tracking

Accurate mileage tracking directly impacts the deductions you can claim during tax season.

5.1. Use the Standard Mileage Rate

The IRS standard mileage rate simplifies deduction calculations:

- Multiply total business miles by the standard rate (e.g., 65.5 cents per mile for 2024).

5.2. Opt for Actual Expenses

Alternatively, you can deduct actual vehicle expenses (e.g., fuel, maintenance, depreciation). However, this method requires detailed documentation of all expenses.

5.3. Keep Detailed Logs

IRS-compliant mileage logs must include:

- Date of the trip.
- Starting location and destination.
- Purpose of the trip.
- Total miles driven.

5.4. Combine with Other Deductions

Mileage deductions can be combined with other travel-related expenses, such as tolls, parking fees, or business-related car insurance.

6. Best Practices for Accurate Mileage Tracking

Adopting best practices ensures your mileage records are accurate, compliant, and easy to manage.

6.1. Automate Whenever Possible

- Use QuickBooks Online's automatic mileage tracking to reduce manual effort.

6.2. Review Logs Regularly

- Set a weekly or monthly schedule to review and categorize trips.

6.3. Keep Supporting Documentation

- Retain receipts for tolls, parking, or other travel-related expenses to complement your mileage records.

6.4. Separate Business and Personal Use

- Dedicate a vehicle to business use if possible, or clearly log mixed-use trips to avoid tax complications.

6.5. Stay Updated on Mileage Rates

- Review IRS announcements annually for updated standard mileage rates.

7. Using Mileage Data for Business Insights

Mileage tracking isn't just for tax deductions—it also provides valuable insights into your business operations.

7.1. Identify Cost Trends

- Analyze mileage reports to identify travel-heavy periods or high-cost routes.

7.2. Optimize Travel Routes

- Use mileage data to plan more efficient routes, saving time and fuel.

7.3. Evaluate Vehicle Usage

- Determine whether your business could benefit from additional vehicles or fuel-efficient alternatives.

8. Troubleshooting Common Mileage Tracking Issues

Even with automated tools, mileage tracking may occasionally present challenges. Here's how to address them:

8.1. Missing Trips

- **Issue**: GPS fails to detect a trip.
- **Solution**: Manually enter the trip details to ensure completeness.

8.2. Incorrect Mileage

- **Issue**: GPS records incorrect distances due to poor signal.
- **Solution**: Cross-check with online mapping tools and adjust manually if needed.

8.3. Misclassified Trips

- **Issue**: Business trips are accidentally marked as personal.
- **Solution**: Regularly review trip logs and reclassify as necessary.

9. Benefits of Using QuickBooks Online for Mileage Tracking

QuickBooks Online streamlines mileage tracking, offering significant benefits for businesses:

- **Accuracy**: GPS tracking ensures precise mileage records.
- **Efficiency**: Automated tools reduce manual entry and save time.
- **Compliance**: IRS-compliant logs protect you during audits.
- **Insights**: Mileage reports provide valuable data for financial planning.

Mileage tracking is a vital part of managing business expenses, maximizing tax deductions, and maintaining financial compliance. QuickBooks Online's mileage tracking tools make the process simple, accurate, and efficient. By automating trip logging, categorizing mileage correctly, and generating detailed reports, you can take control of your travel expenses and make informed financial decisions.

With a solid understanding of mileage tracking, you're now equipped to handle one of the most overlooked yet impactful aspects of expense management. Let's continue exploring how QuickBooks Online can simplify and optimize your financial workflows in the next chapter!

CHAPTER 8
BOOSTING EFFICIENCY WITH APP INTEGRATIONS

In today's fast-paced business environment, efficiency is key. Integrating third-party apps with QuickBooks Online can help streamline workflows, reduce manual tasks, and improve accuracy across various aspects of your business. From payment processors to inventory management systems, these integrations allow you to manage operations more effectively while keeping your financial data centralized and organized.

In this chapter, we'll explore how app integrations can enhance your QuickBooks Online experience. First, we'll introduce some of the **Popular Apps for Small Businesses**, including PayPal, Shopify, and Square. These tools connect seamlessly with Quick-Books to automate tasks like payment processing, e-commerce sales tracking, and point-of-sale operations.

Next, we'll dive into **Managing Inventory**, highlighting apps that provide real-time updates on stock levels, track orders, and sync seamlessly with QuickBooks Online. Whether you're a retailer, wholesaler, or service provider, managing your inventory efficiently is critical to meeting customer demands and optimizing cash flow.

Finally, we'll discuss **Troubleshooting Sync Issues**, a common challenge when working with multiple integrated platforms. You'll learn how to identify and resolve syncing errors, ensuring your systems remain accurate and reliable.

By leveraging app integrations, you can expand the capabilities of QuickBooks Online, saving time and effort while improving your overall business performance. Let's get started and discover how these tools can take your efficiency to the next level!

Popular Apps for Small Businesses: PayPal, Shopify, Square, and More

Running a small business requires juggling multiple tasks, from tracking sales and processing payments to managing inventory and generating financial reports. Integrating popular apps with QuickBooks Online can significantly reduce the time spent on these tasks by automating processes and providing real-time insights into your business operations. Apps like PayPal, Shopify, Square, and others are designed to work seamlessly with Quick-Books Online, offering a streamlined experience for managing payments, sales, and more.

In this chapter, we'll explore the benefits of integrating these popular apps, how they can enhance your QuickBooks Online workflow, and tips for maximizing their potential.

1. Why Integrate Apps with QuickBooks Online?

Integrating apps with QuickBooks Online provides numerous benefits for small businesses:

1.1. Automation

- Reduces manual data entry by syncing transactions directly from the app to QuickBooks Online.
- Automatically categorizes transactions, saving time during bookkeeping and reconciliation.

1.2. Real-Time Updates

- Provides up-to-date information on sales, payments, and inventory, allowing you to make informed decisions quickly.

1.3. Simplified Processes

- Consolidates data from multiple platforms into QuickBooks Online, creating a centralized hub for financial management.

1.4. Improved Accuracy

- Minimizes errors by eliminating manual data entry and ensuring that transactions are recorded consistently.

2. PayPal Integration with QuickBooks Online

2.1. Overview of PayPal

PayPal is one of the most widely used payment processors for online transactions. It's ideal for small businesses that sell products or services online or accept payments from clients around the world.

2.2. Benefits of Integration

- Syncs sales and transaction data automatically with QuickBooks Online.
- Separates PayPal fees from income for accurate financial reporting.
- Handles multi-currency transactions seamlessly.

2.3. How to Integrate PayPal with QuickBooks Online

1. **Access the Apps Tab**

- Go to the **Apps** section in QuickBooks Online and search for "PayPal."

2. Install the PayPal App

- Follow the prompts to connect your PayPal account to Quick-Books Online.

3. Configure Settings

- Choose how transactions are categorized and mapped in QuickBooks Online.

4. Sync Transactions

- PayPal transactions, including payments received and fees, will sync automatically, appearing in the Banking tab for review.

3. Shopify Integration with QuickBooks Online

3.1. Overview of Shopify

Shopify is a leading e-commerce platform that enables small businesses to create online stores, manage products, and process orders.

3.2. Benefits of Integration

- Syncs sales data, tax information, and shipping fees directly with QuickBooks Online.
- Tracks inventory and updates stock levels in real time.
- Generates reports that combine Shopify sales with overall financial data in QuickBooks.

3.3. How to Integrate Shopify with QuickBooks Online

1. Search for Shopify in the App Marketplace

- Navigate to the QuickBooks Online **Apps** section and find the Shopify app.

2. Connect Your Shopify Store

- Log in to your Shopify account and authorize the connection.

3. Map Data Fields

- Match Shopify data fields, such as product categories and sales tax, with corresponding QuickBooks Online categories.

4. Enable Automatic Sync

- Sales, refunds, and shipping costs will sync automatically, ensuring your records are always up to date.

4. Square Integration with QuickBooks Online

4.1. Overview of Square

Square is a popular point-of-sale (POS) system used by small businesses to process in-person payments and manage sales.

4.2. Benefits of Integration

- Transfers sales data, payment methods, and tips directly into QuickBooks Online.
- Syncs inventory updates in real time, reflecting changes from in-store transactions.
- Separates Square fees for accurate expense reporting.

4.3. How to Integrate Square with QuickBooks Online

1. **Install the Sync with Square App**

- Go to the **Apps** section in QuickBooks Online and search for "Sync with Square."

2. **Connect Your Square Account**

- Log in to your Square account and allow integration with QuickBooks Online.

3. **Adjust Settings**

- Configure syncing preferences, such as which accounts to use for recording sales and fees.

4. **Monitor Syncs**

- Transactions from Square will sync daily, appearing in Quick-Books for categorization and reconciliation.

5. Additional Popular Apps for Small Businesses

5.1. Stripe

- **Use Case**: Online payment processing.
- **Benefits**:

- Syncs transactions, fees, and multi-currency payments with QuickBooks Online.
- Automates revenue recognition for subscription-based businesses.

5.2. Etsy

- **Use Case**: Selling handmade or vintage products.
- **Benefits**:
- Syncs Etsy sales, fees, and shipping costs directly with QuickBooks Online.
- Provides insights into profit margins for each product.

5.3. Amazon

- **Use Case**: E-commerce for third-party sellers.
- **Benefits**:
- Integrates Amazon sales data, including fees and refunds, with QuickBooks Online.
- Simplifies inventory tracking and tax reporting for online merchants.

5.4. TSheets (Now QuickBooks Time)

- **Use Case**: Time tracking for payroll and project management.
- **Benefits**:
- Tracks employee hours and syncs data with QuickBooks Payroll.
- Allocates labor costs to specific projects for detailed profitability analysis.

5.5. Expensify

- **Use Case**: Expense management and reimbursement.
- **Benefits**:
- Automatically imports receipts and expense reports into QuickBooks Online.
- Simplifies reimbursement workflows for employees.

6. Maximizing the Benefits of App Integrations

6.1. Centralize Your Data

- Use QuickBooks Online as the central hub for financial data, integrating all relevant apps to reduce duplication and ensure consistency.

6.2. Regularly Review Sync Settings

- Periodically review app settings to ensure transactions are categorized correctly and updates are syncing as expected.

6.3. Leverage App Reports

- Utilize reports from integrated apps to gain deeper insights into sales trends, customer behavior, and inventory performance.

6.4. Train Your Team

- Provide training for employees on how to use integrated apps effectively, ensuring consistency and reducing errors.

7. Troubleshooting Common Integration Issues

While integrations simplify workflows, occasional issues may arise. Here's how to handle them:

7.1. Duplicate Transactions

- **Cause**: Transactions sync from multiple sources.
- **Solution**: Identify duplicates in the Banking tab and exclude one of the entries.

7.2. Sync Failures

- **Cause**: Connectivity issues or outdated credentials.
- **Solution**: Reconnect the app and verify login details.

7.3. Data Mismatches

- **Cause**: Inconsistent data mapping between the app and QuickBooks Online.
- **Solution**: Adjust mapping settings to align categories correctly.

8. The Future of App Integrations

As technology evolves, app integrations will become even more powerful, enabling small businesses to automate more tasks and gain richer insights. Emerging trends include:

- **AI-Driven Automation**: Predictive analytics and smart categorization will further reduce manual effort.
- **Expanded Integrations**: New apps will continue to emerge, offering specialized solutions for unique business needs.
- **Deeper Insights**: Integrated platforms will provide advanced reporting, combining data from multiple sources for comprehensive analysis.

Integrating apps like PayPal, Shopify, Square, and others with QuickBooks Online transforms how small businesses manage their operations. These integrations streamline payment processing, inventory management, and sales tracking, saving time and improving accuracy.

By leveraging the full potential of these tools, you can focus more on growing your business and less on administrative tasks.

Whether you're managing e-commerce sales, tracking point-of-sale transactions, or processing online payments, QuickBooks Online's compatibility with popular apps makes it the ultimate platform for small business success. Start exploring these integrations today to unlock new levels of efficiency and productivity!

Managing Inventory: Tools for Real-Time Updates

Effective inventory management is essential for businesses that sell products. Whether you run a retail store, an online shop, or a wholesale business, keeping track of inventory levels, managing stock, and forecasting demand are critical tasks. Poor inventory management can lead to stockouts, overstocking, lost sales, or wasted resources. With QuickBooks Online and its integrated tools, you can manage inventory in real-time, streamline operations, and maintain optimal stock levels.

This chapter explores how QuickBooks Online's inventory management features and app integrations help businesses track inventory accurately, gain real-time updates, and make informed decisions to improve efficiency and profitability.

1. Why Real-Time Inventory Management Matters

Inventory is one of the most valuable assets for product-based businesses. Real-time inventory management ensures that your stock levels are always accurate, helping you avoid common challenges.

1.1. Benefits of Real-Time Inventory Management

- **Improved Accuracy**: Eliminates errors caused by manual tracking or delayed updates.
- **Optimized Stock Levels**: Ensures you have the right amount of stock to meet customer demand without overstocking.
- **Enhanced Customer Satisfaction**: Reduces the risk of stock-outs and backorders.
- **Better Financial Planning**: Provides accurate data for budgeting, forecasting, and decision-making.

1.2. Challenges Without Real-Time Updates

- Overstocking leads to tied-up capital and higher storage costs.
- Stockouts result in lost sales and disappointed customers.
- Inaccurate inventory data can cause discrepancies in financial reports and tax filings.

2. Inventory Management Features in QuickBooks Online

QuickBooks Online includes robust inventory management tools that simplify tracking and reporting.

2.1. Tracking Inventory Levels

1. **Adding Inventory Items**
- Navigate to **Sales > Products and Services**.
- Click **New > Inventory** and enter details such as item name, SKU, purchase cost, and selling price.

2. **Real-Time Updates**
- Each time you sell, purchase, or adjust stock, QuickBooks updates your inventory levels automatically.

3. Low-Stock Alerts

- Set minimum stock thresholds, and QuickBooks will notify you when it's time to reorder.

2.2. Managing Non-Inventory Items

For businesses that sell services or non-stock items (e.g., materials consumed during projects), QuickBooks allows you to track these separately to maintain accurate expense records.

2.3. Generating Inventory Reports

1. Inventory Valuation Summary

- View the total value of your inventory on hand, including quantities, costs, and potential sales value.

2. Sales by Product/Service

- Analyze which products generate the most revenue or require frequent restocking.

3. Inventory Quantity on Hand

- Monitor stock levels and plan reorders effectively.

3. Real-Time Inventory Integrations

QuickBooks Online can be integrated with specialized inventory management apps for businesses with complex needs or high transaction volumes.

3.1. Popular Inventory Apps

- **Shopify**: For e-commerce businesses, Shopify syncs inventory levels across online stores and QuickBooks.
- **Cin7**: A robust inventory management solution for wholesalers and multi-channel retailers.
- **TradeGecko (QuickBooks Commerce)**: Tracks inventory across multiple sales channels and warehouses.
- **DEAR Inventory**: Offers advanced features like batch tracking, manufacturing workflows, and cost analysis.

3.2. Syncing Inventory Data

1. Install the App

- Navigate to the **Apps** section in QuickBooks Online and find the desired inventory app.

2. Connect Your Accounts

- Log in to the app and authorize integration with QuickBooks Online.

3. Set Up Data Mapping

- Match fields like product categories, stock locations, and transaction types between QuickBooks and the app.

4. Enable Automatic Updates

- Inventory quantities, sales orders, and purchase orders will sync in real-time.

4. Optimizing Inventory with Real-Time Tools

Real-time inventory management tools help businesses operate more efficiently and profitably.

4.1. Stock Replenishment

- **Low-Stock Notifications**: Receive alerts when stock levels reach reorder points.
- **Automated Purchase Orders**: Set rules to automatically create purchase orders when stock levels fall below minimum thresholds.

4.2. Inventory Forecasting

- Analyze historical sales data to predict future demand.
- Use seasonality trends to plan for peak periods and avoid stockouts.

4.3. Multi-Location Tracking

- Monitor inventory across multiple warehouses, retail stores, or sales channels.
- Assign inventory to specific locations and track transfers between them.

4.4. Batch and Serial Number Tracking

- For businesses requiring detailed tracking, QuickBooks and integrated apps allow you to record batch numbers or serial numbers for each item.

5. Best Practices for Real-Time Inventory Management

Adopting best practices ensures that your inventory system operates smoothly and provides reliable data.

5.1. Regular Audits

- Conduct physical inventory counts periodically to verify that on-hand quantities match system records.

5.2. Categorize Products

- Organize inventory by categories or types (e.g., by product line, size, or color) to streamline management.

5.3. Train Employees

- Ensure all staff involved in inventory handling understand how to record transactions and use the inventory management system correctly.

5.4. Monitor Turnover Rates

- Use inventory turnover ratios to identify slow-moving or obsolete stock, allowing you to focus on high-demand items.

6. Common Challenges and Solutions

While QuickBooks Online simplifies inventory management, challenges can arise. Here's how to address them:

6.1. Inconsistent Updates

- **Cause**: Delayed entry of sales or purchases.
- **Solution**: Use real-time integrations and train staff to update inventory promptly.

6.2. Stock Discrepancies

- **Cause**: Errors during physical counts or transactions.
- **Solution**: Reconcile inventory records regularly and investigate discrepancies immediately.

6.3. Overselling

- **Cause**: Inventory not syncing across multiple sales channels.
- **Solution**: Integrate QuickBooks with inventory apps that support multi-channel sales tracking.

7. Leveraging Inventory Data for Strategic Decisions

Real-time inventory data provides insights that go beyond stock levels, helping you make strategic business decisions.

7.1. Identifying Best Sellers

- Use sales reports to identify high-performing products and allocate resources accordingly.

7.2. Managing Supplier Relationships

- Monitor vendor performance based on delivery times, quality, and pricing.

7.3. Pricing Strategies

- Use cost and sales data to optimize pricing for maximum profitability.

7.4. Expansion Opportunities

- Evaluate whether current inventory systems can support growth into new locations or sales channels.

8. Future Trends in Inventory Management

As technology evolves, inventory management tools are becoming even more sophisticated.

8.1. Artificial Intelligence

- AI-powered tools analyze sales trends and recommend optimal stock levels.

8.2. Internet of Things (IoT)

- Smart sensors and RFID tags provide real-time tracking of inventory in warehouses.

8.3. Blockchain

- Blockchain technology enhances transparency and traceability across supply chains.

Managing inventory in real-time is essential for any business that sells products. QuickBooks Online, combined with powerful integrations, provides the tools needed to track inventory levels, monitor stock movements, and optimize replenishment processes. By adopting real-time inventory management, you can improve accuracy, reduce costs, and ensure you always have the right products available for your customers.

With a clear understanding of these tools and best practices, you're well-equipped to manage inventory efficiently and make data-driven decisions that drive business success. Let's continue exploring how QuickBooks Online's features can streamline your operations and enhance your financial management!

Troubleshooting Sync Issues: Keeping Your System Running Smoothly

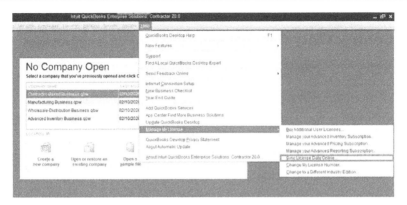

Syncing data between QuickBooks Online and integrated apps is crucial for maintaining accurate records and seamless business operations. However, occasional sync issues can arise, disrupting workflows and causing discrepancies in your financial data. Understanding how to troubleshoot these problems effectively ensures your system remains reliable, and your data stays consistent across platforms.

In this chapter, we'll delve into common sync issues, their causes, and step-by-step solutions. We'll also provide best practices for preventing sync problems, enabling you to maintain a smooth, error-free system.

1. Why Sync Issues Matter

Sync issues can lead to data discrepancies, missed transactions, or duplicate entries, which may affect your financial reports and decision-making. Addressing these problems promptly ensures:

- **Accuracy**: Prevents mismatches between your QuickBooks Online account and integrated apps.
- **Efficiency**: Reduces time spent on manual corrections.
- **Compliance**: Ensures tax and financial reports are accurate and audit-ready.

2. Common Causes of Sync Issues

Understanding the root causes of sync issues can help you identify and resolve problems quickly.

2.1. Connectivity Problems

- Poor internet connection or server outages can interrupt sync processes.
- Temporary network glitches may cause partial or failed data transfers.

2.2. Incorrect Settings

- Mismatched data fields between QuickBooks Online and the integrated app can result in sync errors.
- Misconfigured settings, such as tax codes or account mappings, may cause transactions to fail.

2.3. Outdated Software

- Using an outdated version of QuickBooks Online or an integrated app may create compatibility issues.
- Apps may require periodic updates to align with QuickBooks Online's system updates.

2.4. Duplicate Data Entries

- Duplicate entries in either QuickBooks Online or the app can cause conflicts during syncing.
- Improper data import processes may create overlapping records.

2.5. Permissions and Access

- Insufficient permissions in QuickBooks Online or the app may prevent data syncing.
- Multiple user roles with conflicting settings can disrupt sync processes.

3. Troubleshooting Sync Issues

When sync issues arise, follow these steps to identify and resolve the problem.

3.1. Verify Internet Connectivity

1.   Check Your Network

- Ensure your internet connection is stable and has sufficient bandwidth.

2.   Restart Devices

- Restart your computer, router, or modem to refresh the connection.

3.2. Check Integration Settings

1.   Access App Settings

- Navigate to the app's integration settings in QuickBooks Online or the app itself.

2.   Review Field Mappings

- Ensure data fields (e.g., customer names, account codes) are mapped correctly between QuickBooks and the app.

3.   Verify Sync Schedule

- Confirm that automatic sync is enabled and set to the correct frequency (e.g., daily or hourly).

3.3. Update Software

1.   Check for Updates

- Visit the app marketplace or the app's website to verify that you're using the latest version.

2.   Install Updates

- Update both QuickBooks Online and the integrated app to resolve compatibility issues.

3.4. Resolve Duplicate Entries

1.   Run a Duplicate Check

- Use QuickBooks Online's search or filter tools to identify duplicate transactions.

2.   Delete or Merge Records

- Remove duplicates or merge similar records to maintain consistency.

3.5. Review User Permissions

1.   Check Access Levels

- Ensure all users involved in the sync process have the necessary permissions.

2.   Align Roles

- Update roles in QuickBooks Online and the app to prevent conflicts.

3.6. Test the Sync

1.   Perform a Manual Sync

- Trigger a manual sync to test if the problem persists.

2.   Monitor Logs

- Review error logs in QuickBooks Online or the app for detailed information about failed transactions.

4. Resolving Specific Sync Errors

Here's how to address some of the most common sync errors:

4.1. Error: "Transaction Failed to Sync"

- **Cause**: Mismatched fields or missing data.
- **Solution**:
    1.   Check required fields in both QuickBooks Online and the app.
    2.   Complete missing information, such as customer names or item details.

4.2. Error: "Account Not Found"

- **Cause**: Account mappings are incorrect or unavailable.
- **Solution**:
    1.   Go to **Settings > Chart of Accounts** in QuickBooks Online.
    2.   Map the missing account to the correct category.

4.3. Error: "App Not Authorized"

- **Cause**: Integration permissions were revoked or expired.

- **Solution**:
    1. Reauthorize the app by logging into your QuickBooks Online account.
    2. Navigate to **Settings > Apps** and reconnect the app.

4.4. Error: "Duplicate Transaction Detected"

- **Cause**: The app attempts to sync a transaction already recorded in QuickBooks Online.
- **Solution**:
    1. Review the transaction history in QuickBooks Online.
    2. Delete or exclude duplicates from the sync process.

5. Preventing Future Sync Issues

Taking proactive steps can help you avoid sync problems and maintain a smooth workflow.

5.1. Regularly Update Software

- Schedule periodic checks for software updates and install them promptly to maintain compatibility.

5.2. Monitor Sync Logs

- Review sync logs regularly to identify and address issues before they escalate.

5.3. Clean Up Data

- Periodically audit and clean up records in QuickBooks Online and connected apps to prevent duplicates and inconsistencies.

5.4. Use Reliable Integrations

- Choose well-supported apps with robust integration capabilities and positive user reviews.

5.5. Schedule Syncs During Downtime

- Schedule large sync operations during low-traffic periods to reduce the risk of interruptions.

6. Leveraging Support Resources

When troubleshooting on your own doesn't resolve the issue, turn to support resources for additional help.

6.1. QuickBooks Online Support

- Access the **Help** menu in QuickBooks Online for articles, FAQs, and tutorials.
- Contact QuickBooks support directly for assistance with persistent sync issues.

6.2. App Support Teams

- Most integrated apps offer dedicated support for QuickBooks users. Reach out to their helpdesk or live chat for guidance.

6.3. Community Forums

- Visit the QuickBooks Community or app-specific forums to find solutions from other users who've experienced similar issues.

7. Benefits of a Smooth Sync System

By maintaining a reliable sync system, you can enjoy several advantages:

- **Time Savings**: Eliminates the need for manual data entry and corrections.
- **Improved Accuracy**: Ensures your financial records and reports are always up-to-date and error-free.
- **Seamless Workflows**: Streamlines processes, allowing you to focus on strategic business tasks.
- **Enhanced Decision-Making**: Provides real-time insights across platforms for better business decisions.

8. Case Study: Troubleshooting Success

A small e-commerce business integrating Shopify with QuickBooks Online encountered frequent sync errors due to outdated app versions and mismatched tax codes. By:

1. Updating both platforms to their latest versions,
2. Reconfiguring tax code mappings,
3. Performing a manual sync and monitoring error logs,

the business resolved its sync issues, enabling real-time inventory tracking and accurate sales data reporting. This streamlined their operations and improved customer satisfaction by reducing order delays.

Sync issues can disrupt your workflow and create financial discrepancies, but with the right approach, they're manageable and preventable. QuickBooks Online's robust tools, combined with careful monitoring and proactive troubleshooting, help you keep your system running smoothly. By understanding common sync problems, implementing best practices, and leveraging support resources, you can maintain a reliable and efficient integration system that supports your business's growth.

With your sync processes under control, you can focus on maximizing the value of QuickBooks Online and its integrations to enhance your business's financial management and operational efficiency.

BOOK 3

ADVANCED FEATURES AND TROUBLESHOOTING

Welcome to **Book 3: Advanced Features and Troubleshooting**, where we explore the powerful tools and solutions that QuickBooks Online offers to streamline complex business processes. This book is designed for users ready to go beyond the basics and unlock the full potential of QuickBooks Online to manage advanced tasks and address challenges with confidence.

In this book, we'll begin with **Payroll and Employee Management**, a critical area for businesses with staff. You'll learn how to set up payroll systems, automate employee payments, and ensure compliance with state and federal tax filing requirements. These tools simplify payroll management while saving time and reducing errors.

Next, we'll dive into **Inventory and Budgeting**, where you'll discover strategies for tracking stock levels, managing costs, and setting up effective budgets. Learn how to prevent stockouts, configure low-stock alerts, and use budgets to monitor financial performance and achieve your business goals.

In **Advanced Reporting and Analytics**, we'll show you how to customize reports, forecast growth, and use audit logs to maintain data integrity. These features empower you to transform raw financial data into actionable insights for strategic planning and business growth.

Finally, **Troubleshooting and Efficiency Hacks** will guide you through resolving common errors, implementing time-saving keyboard shortcuts, and following best practices for maintaining organized bookkeeping. Whether you're addressing technical glitches or enhancing your workflow, this chapter will provide the tools and techniques you need to stay productive and audit-ready.

By the end of this book, you'll be equipped to leverage Quick-Books Online's advanced features while confidently trouble-shooting any issues that arise. Let's embark on this journey to master the tools and strategies that will elevate your financial management capabilities!

CHAPTER 9
PAYROLL AND EMPLOYEE MANAGEMENT

Payroll and employee management are vital components of running a business with a team. Ensuring that your employees are paid accurately and on time, while staying compliant with tax regulations, is critical for maintaining morale and avoiding legal issues. QuickBooks Online's payroll tools make managing these tasks more straightforward, allowing you to focus on growing your business.

In this chapter, we'll guide you through the key aspects of payroll and employee management using QuickBooks Online. First, we'll cover **Setting Up Payroll**, including how to configure pay schedules, calculate taxes, and ensure compliance with state and federal regulations. A properly configured payroll system sets the foundation for smooth and accurate employee payments.

Next, we'll delve into **Automating Employee Payments**, demonstrating how to use direct deposits to save time and reduce manual errors. Automated payments not only streamline payroll processing but also enhance employee satisfaction by ensuring timely payments.

Finally, we'll explore the essentials of **Tax Filing Basics**, where you'll learn how to file payroll taxes with confidence. QuickBooks Online simplifies this process by automating calculations, generating necessary forms, and helping you meet deadlines for both state and federal payroll tax filings.

By the end of this chapter, you'll have a clear understanding of how to use QuickBooks Online to manage payroll efficiently, stay compliant with tax laws, and build trust with your employees through accurate and timely payments. Let's get started!

Setting Up Payroll: Taxes, Pay Schedules, and Compliance

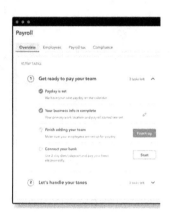

Payroll management is one of the most crucial aspects of running a business with employees. Ensuring that employees are paid accurately and on time while complying with tax regulations is not only a legal obligation but also essential for maintaining employee trust and morale. QuickBooks Online provides robust payroll tools that simplify the process, allowing you to set up and manage payroll efficiently.

This chapter will guide you through the step-by-step process of setting up payroll in QuickBooks Online, including configuring pay schedules, calculating taxes, and ensuring compliance with state and federal regulations.

1. The Importance of a Properly Configured Payroll System

A well-structured payroll system is the backbone of effective employee management. Here's why it matters:

1.1. Employee Satisfaction

- Timely and accurate payments build trust and satisfaction among employees, boosting productivity and retention.

1.2. Legal Compliance

- Payroll systems ensure compliance with labor laws, tax regulations, and reporting requirements.

1.3. Operational Efficiency

- Automated payroll systems reduce administrative burden, allowing you to focus on strategic business activities.

2. Preparing to Set Up Payroll

Before setting up payroll in QuickBooks Online, gather the necessary information:

2.1. Employee Information

- Collect the following details from each employee:
- Full name, Social Security Number (SSN), and address.
- Tax filing status and allowances (from Form W-4).
- Pay rate, bonuses, or additional compensation details.

2.2. Business Information

- Ensure your business details are accurate and up-to-date:
- Employer Identification Number (EIN).
- State and federal tax identification numbers.
- Bank account information for payroll transactions.

2.3. Payroll History

- If you're switching to QuickBooks mid-year, gather previous payroll data for accurate year-to-date reporting.

3. Setting Up Payroll in QuickBooks Online

QuickBooks Online's payroll setup wizard simplifies the process, guiding you step by step.

3.1. Accessing Payroll Setup

1. **Navigate to Payroll**

- Go to the left-hand menu in QuickBooks Online and select **Payroll**.

2. Choose a Payroll Plan

- Select a plan that meets your business needs (e.g., Core, Premium, or Elite).

3.2. Adding Employees

1. Add Employee Details

- Enter each employee's name, SSN, and contact details.

2. Set Compensation

- Specify hourly rates, salaries, or other pay structures.

3. Input Tax Information

- Enter tax details from Form W-4, including filing status and additional withholdings.

3.3. Configuring Pay Schedules

1. Select Pay Frequency

- Choose how often employees are paid (e.g., weekly, bi-weekly, semi-monthly, or monthly).

2. Set Pay Dates

- Define the pay period and corresponding pay date.

3. Assign Schedules to Employees

- Link each employee to their appropriate pay schedule.

3.4. Adding Benefits and Deductions

- Include employee benefits such as health insurance, retirement contributions, or flexible spending accounts.
- Set up deductions for garnishments, child support, or other obligations.

4. Setting Up Payroll Taxes

Payroll taxes are a critical component of compliance. QuickBooks Online automates tax calculations and filings to reduce errors and save time.

4.1. Configuring Federal Taxes

1. Employer Identification Number (EIN)

- Ensure your EIN is correctly entered in QuickBooks Online.

2. Federal Tax Rates

- QuickBooks calculates Social Security, Medicare, and federal unemployment taxes (FUTA) automatically.

4.2. Setting Up State Taxes

1. State Tax ID Numbers

- Enter your state unemployment insurance (SUI) account number and other state tax details.

2. State Tax Rates

- QuickBooks updates state tax rates automatically but requires initial setup.

4.3. Local Taxes

- For businesses in areas with local taxes, add the relevant information during setup.

4.4. Automating Tax Payments

- Enable automated tax payments and filings to ensure timely compliance with state and federal deadlines.

5. Running Payroll

Once setup is complete, running payroll in QuickBooks Online is simple and efficient.

5.1. Reviewing Employee Hours

1. Input Hours Worked

- Enter hours manually or import them from a time-tracking app like QuickBooks Time.

2. Verify Overtime

- Confirm that overtime hours and rates are calculated correctly.

5.2. Previewing Payroll

1. Review Paychecks

- Check individual paychecks for accuracy, including deductions, taxes, and benefits.

2. Verify Totals

- Ensure that total payroll amounts match expected expenses.

5.3. Submitting Payroll

1. Approve and Submit

- Once reviewed, approve and submit payroll.

2. Process Payments

- Payments are processed via direct deposit or printed checks, depending on your setup.

6. Ensuring Payroll Compliance

Compliance with labor laws and tax regulations is critical for avoiding penalties and maintaining a positive reputation.

6.1. Filing Payroll Taxes

- QuickBooks Online generates and files payroll tax forms (e.g., Form 941, Form W-2) automatically if enabled.
- Ensure all tax filings are submitted by the deadlines to avoid penalties.

6.2. Recordkeeping

- Maintain detailed payroll records for at least three years as required by the Fair Labor Standards Act (FLSA).

6.3. Audit Preparation

- Use QuickBooks Online reports to prepare for payroll audits and ensure compliance with labor laws.

7. Troubleshooting Payroll Issues

Even with a well-configured system, payroll challenges may arise. Here's how to address them:

7.1. Incorrect Deductions

- **Solution**: Double-check benefit and tax settings in the employee profile.

7.2. Missing Payments

- **Solution**: Verify bank account details and contact QuickBooks support if necessary.

7.3. Tax Filing Errors

- **Solution**: Review tax setup and amend filings promptly if errors are identified.

8. Best Practices for Payroll Management

Implement these best practices to ensure smooth payroll operations:

8.1. Regularly Update Employee Information

- Keep employee profiles current to reflect changes in pay rates, benefits, or tax details.

8.2. Automate Processes

- Use automation for tax filings, direct deposits, and recurring benefits deductions to minimize manual effort.

8.3. Review Payroll Reports

- Generate payroll summary reports to monitor expenses and identify discrepancies.

8.4. Stay Informed

- Monitor changes in tax laws and labor regulations that may impact payroll processes.

Setting up payroll in QuickBooks Online ensures your employees are paid accurately and on time while keeping your business compliant with tax regulations. By following the steps outlined in this chapter, you can configure pay schedules, automate tax calculations, and streamline payroll operations. A well-structured payroll system not only saves time but also fosters trust with your employees and protects your business from compliance risks.

Now that you've mastered payroll setup, let's explore how automation can further simplify employee payments in the next section!

Automating Employee Payments: Save Time with Direct Deposits

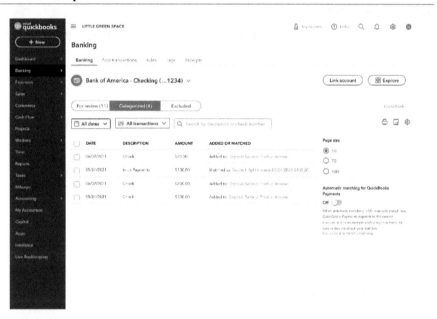

Managing employee payments is one of the most critical and time-sensitive responsibilities for any business owner. Employees rely on timely and accurate payments, and businesses need efficient systems to ensure payroll runs smoothly. Automating employee payments using direct deposits is an excellent way to save time, reduce errors, and improve employee satisfaction. QuickBooks Online provides robust features to streamline this process, making it a reliable solution for businesses of all sizes.

In this chapter, we'll explore the benefits of automating employee payments with direct deposits, guide you through the setup process in QuickBooks Online, and share best practices for maintaining an efficient payroll system.

1. Why Automate Employee Payments?

Automating payments through direct deposit offers significant advantages for both employers and employees.

1.1. Time Savings

- Eliminates the need to print, sign, and distribute physical checks.
- Speeds up payroll processing by automating repetitive tasks.

1.2. Accuracy and Reliability

- Reduces human errors associated with manual calculations and check preparation.
- Ensures employees receive payments directly into their accounts without delays.

1.3. Cost Efficiency

- Saves money on check printing, postage, and administrative costs.

1.4. Employee Satisfaction

- Employees appreciate the convenience and security of direct deposits, as funds are available immediately on payday.

1.5. Environmental Impact

- Reduces paper waste associated with physical checks.

2. Setting Up Direct Deposits in QuickBooks Online

QuickBooks Online simplifies the process of setting up direct deposits, ensuring that your payroll operations run smoothly.

2.1. Prerequisites for Direct Deposit

Before setting up direct deposits, ensure you have the following:

- **Business Bank Account**: A verified account for transferring payroll funds.
- **Employee Bank Details**: Employees' bank account numbers and routing numbers.

- **Payroll Subscription**: An active QuickBooks Online Payroll subscription.

2.2. Enabling Direct Deposit

1. **Access Payroll Settings**
- Log in to QuickBooks Online and navigate to **Payroll Settings**.

2. **Set Up Your Business Bank Account**
- Provide your business bank account details and verify the account through a micro-deposit verification process.

3. **Add Employee Bank Details**
- In the employee profile, input the employee's bank account type (checking or savings), account number, and routing number.

4. **Enable Direct Deposit**
- Turn on the direct deposit option for each employee.

2.3. Authorizing Transactions

- Employees must sign a direct deposit authorization form, granting permission for electronic payments.

3. Running Payroll with Direct Deposits

Once direct deposit is set up, running payroll is a streamlined process in QuickBooks Online.

3.1. Enter Payroll Information

1. **Review Employee Hours**
- Enter hours worked, overtime, or paid time off (PTO) if applicable.

2. **Verify Deductions**
- Check for benefits deductions, tax withholdings, and other adjustments.

3.2. Preview Payroll

- QuickBooks Online calculates gross pay, deductions, and net pay automatically. Review the totals to ensure accuracy.

3.3. Submit Payroll

1. Approve Payroll

- Confirm that all details are correct and approve the payroll.

2. Process Payments

- QuickBooks will initiate direct deposits, ensuring employees receive funds on payday.

3.4. Notifications

- Employees can receive email notifications confirming that their pay has been deposited.

4. Benefits of Automating Direct Deposits

4.1. Seamless Payment Process

- Direct deposits ensure a seamless transfer of funds from your business account to employees' accounts, reducing administrative burdens.

4.2. Enhanced Security

- Electronic transfers are more secure than physical checks, reducing the risk of theft or loss.

4.3. Real-Time Payroll Tracking

- QuickBooks Online provides real-time tracking of payroll transactions, offering insights into payment statuses.

4.4. Compliance Support

- Automated payroll systems help ensure compliance with labor laws and tax regulations, reducing the risk of penalties.

5. Troubleshooting Common Direct Deposit Issues

While direct deposits are efficient, occasional challenges may arise. Here's how to address them:

5.1. Employee Didn't Receive Payment

- **Cause**: Incorrect bank details.
- **Solution**: Verify the employee's account and routing numbers, and correct any errors.

5.2. Payment Delays

- **Cause**: Insufficient funds in the business account.
- **Solution**: Ensure your account has sufficient funds before running payroll.

5.3. Duplicate Payments

- **Cause**: Errors during payroll submission.
- **Solution**: Void duplicate payments in QuickBooks Online and contact support if needed.

5.4. Bank Holidays

- **Cause**: Payroll submitted on a bank holiday.
- **Solution**: Schedule payroll processing at least two business days before payday to account for holidays.

6. Best Practices for Automating Employee Payments

To ensure a smooth and reliable direct deposit process, follow these best practices:

6.1. Verify Employee Information

- Double-check bank details and ensure employee profiles are complete and accurate.

6.2. Schedule Payroll in Advance

- Submit payroll at least two business days before payday to avoid delays.

6.3. Monitor Bank Balances

- Maintain sufficient funds in your business account to cover payroll and associated taxes.

6.4. Use Payroll Reports

- Generate payroll reports to track expenses, review trends, and ensure accuracy.

6.5. Communicate with Employees

- Inform employees about direct deposit timelines and provide a breakdown of their pay stubs.

7. Advanced Features of QuickBooks Online Payroll

QuickBooks Online Payroll offers advanced features that enhance the direct deposit experience:

7.1. Multiple Pay Schedules

- Create different pay schedules for hourly, salaried, and contract employees.

7.2. Off-Cycle Payments

- Issue bonuses, reimbursements, or corrections outside regular payroll cycles using direct deposits.

7.3. Automated Tax Filing

- QuickBooks Online calculates, withholds, and files payroll taxes automatically, simplifying compliance.

7.4. Employee Self-Service

- Employees can access their pay stubs, tax forms, and payment history via the QuickBooks Workforce portal.

8. Advantages for Employees

Direct deposits offer employees several benefits, including:

- **Convenience**: No need to visit a bank or deposit checks manually.
- **Timely Payments**: Funds are available on payday without delays.
- **Security**: Electronic payments reduce the risk of lost or stolen checks.

- **Transparency**: Employees receive detailed pay stubs outlining earnings, deductions, and taxes.

9. Scaling Payroll Automation as Your Business Grows

As your business expands, automating employee payments ensures scalability and efficiency.

9.1. Managing Larger Teams

- QuickBooks Online Payroll supports businesses with growing employee counts, making it easy to add new team members.

9.2. Handling Multi-State Payroll

- For businesses operating in multiple states, QuickBooks Online simplifies tax compliance and payment processing.

9.3. International Payments

- Use third-party integrations like TransferWise or Payoneer to manage payments for remote or international employees.

Automating employee payments through direct deposits is a smart choice for businesses looking to streamline payroll processes, enhance accuracy, and save time. QuickBooks Online makes it easy to set up and manage direct deposits, ensuring that employees are paid promptly and securely. By adopting automation and following best practices, you can focus on growing your business while maintaining a reliable and efficient payroll system.

With direct deposits in place, you're well-equipped to handle payroll smoothly and professionally. In the next section, we'll explore the fundamentals of tax filing to ensure your business remains compliant with state and federal regulations. Let's continue optimizing your payroll processes!

Tax Filing Basics: Filing State and Federal Payroll Taxes

Filing payroll taxes is one of the most critical responsibilities for businesses with employees. Properly managing state and federal tax filings ensures compliance with legal requirements, prevents costly penalties, and maintains employee trust. QuickBooks Online simplifies this often complex process by automating tax calculations, preparing forms, and submitting filings on your behalf.

In this chapter, we'll explore the fundamentals of payroll tax filing, explain how to handle state and federal requirements, and guide you through using QuickBooks Online to stay compliant and efficient.

1. Understanding Payroll Taxes

Payroll taxes are deductions and contributions required by law, applied to employee wages and employer obligations. They are divided into federal, state, and, in some cases, local taxes.

1.1. Federal Payroll Taxes

Federal taxes include:

- **Social Security Tax**: 6.2% from employees, matched by employers.
- **Medicare Tax**: 1.45% from employees, matched by employers.

- **Federal Unemployment Tax (FUTA)**: Paid solely by employers.

1.2. State Payroll Taxes

State tax requirements vary but may include:

- **State Income Tax**: Withheld from employee wages based on state-specific rates.
- **State Unemployment Tax (SUTA)**: Paid by employers to fund unemployment benefits.

1.3. Local Payroll Taxes

Some localities impose additional taxes, such as city income tax or transit taxes, which must also be withheld and filed.

2. Key Steps in Filing Payroll Taxes

To ensure compliance, follow these essential steps when managing payroll taxes.

2.1. Obtain Tax Identification Numbers

- **Federal EIN**: Register with the IRS to obtain an Employer Identification Number.
- **State Tax ID**: Apply for state-specific employer identification numbers for income tax and unemployment insurance.

2.2. Calculate Taxes

QuickBooks Online automates tax calculations, but it's important to understand the breakdown:

- Employee deductions (e.g., income tax, Social Security, Medicare).
- Employer contributions (e.g., FUTA, SUTA, Social Security, Medicare).

2.3. Withhold Taxes

- Deduct federal, state, and local taxes from employee wages during payroll processing.

2.4. Deposit Taxes

- Use the Electronic Federal Tax Payment System (EFTPS) or state-specific portals to deposit withheld taxes regularly.

2.5. File Tax Forms

- Submit quarterly and annual tax filings, including:
- **Form 941**: Employer's Quarterly Federal Tax Return.
- **Form 940**: Employer's Annual Federal Unemployment Tax Return.
- **State Forms**: Vary by state but typically include income tax and unemployment filings.

3. Filing Federal Payroll Taxes with QuickBooks Online

QuickBooks Online automates federal payroll tax filings, making the process efficient and error-free.

3.1. Automating Federal Tax Payments

1. **Set Up Tax Payments**

- Navigate to **Payroll Settings > Taxes and Forms** and connect to EFTPS.

2. **Schedule Deposits**

- QuickBooks determines deposit frequency based on your tax liability and automatically schedules payments.

3.2. Filing Form 941

- **What It Covers**: Reports Social Security, Medicare, and withheld federal income taxes.
- **How to File**:
  1. QuickBooks Online prepares Form 941 quarterly.
  2. Review the form for accuracy.
  3. Submit electronically through QuickBooks or print and mail if required.

3.3. Filing Form 940

- **What It Covers**: Reports FUTA taxes paid by employers annually.

- **How to File**:
  1. Ensure FUTA payments are up-to-date.
  2. Let QuickBooks Online generate Form 940 at year-end.
  3. Submit the form electronically or via mail.

4. Filing State Payroll Taxes with QuickBooks Online

State tax filings are just as important as federal filings, and QuickBooks Online supports many state systems.

4.1. Configuring State Tax Settings

1. Enter State Tax IDs

- Input your state unemployment insurance (SUI) account number and other applicable IDs.

2. Set Up Withholding Rates

- QuickBooks uses state-provided tax tables to calculate income tax.

4.2. Automating State Tax Payments

- QuickBooks calculates and schedules payments for:
- State income tax withholdings.
- SUTA contributions.
- Other state-specific taxes.

4.3. Filing State Tax Forms

1. Quarterly Filings

- QuickBooks Online generates and submits required state forms based on your schedule.

2. Year-End Filings

- Submit W-2s and state reconciliation forms through QuickBooks Online.

5. Managing Local Payroll Taxes

Local payroll taxes, while less common, must be handled with the same care as federal and state taxes.

5.1. Understanding Local Requirements

- Research local tax laws to identify obligations like city income tax or transit tax.

5.2. Setting Up Local Taxes in QuickBooks

- Add local tax rates in the **Payroll Settings** section.

5.3. Filing Local Tax Forms

- Use QuickBooks to calculate and pay local taxes, and ensure you meet filing deadlines.

6. Best Practices for Payroll Tax Compliance

Adopting best practices can help you avoid common pitfalls and maintain compliance.

6.1. Stay Organized

- Use QuickBooks Online to store tax documents, payment receipts, and filing confirmations.

6.2. Keep Employee Records Up-to-Date

- Ensure employee profiles reflect current tax filing statuses, allowances, and benefits.

6.3. Monitor Deadlines

- QuickBooks provides reminders for deposit and filing deadlines, helping you avoid penalties.

6.4. Reconcile Tax Accounts Regularly

- Compare QuickBooks tax records with bank statements and IRS notices to ensure accuracy.

6.5. Stay Informed

- Keep up with changes to federal, state, and local tax laws that may affect payroll processing.

7. Troubleshooting Payroll Tax Issues

When issues arise, QuickBooks Online provides tools to resolve them quickly.

7.1. Missed Payments

- **Solution**: Use QuickBooks to calculate late fees and penalties, and schedule the missed payment immediately.

7.2. Incorrect Filings

- **Solution**: Amend the incorrect tax form using QuickBooks Online or consult a tax professional.

7.3. Tax Notices

- **Solution**: Upload the notice to QuickBooks, and their payroll tax experts can help resolve the issue.

8. Leveraging Professional Help

For complex payroll tax situations, consider seeking expert assistance.

8.1. QuickBooks Payroll Tax Support

- QuickBooks Online offers payroll tax support for resolving tax notices and filing errors.

8.2. Hiring a Payroll Specialist

- For larger businesses, a payroll specialist or CPA can provide personalized guidance.

9. Advantages of Using QuickBooks Online for Tax Filing

QuickBooks Online simplifies payroll tax filing in several ways:

- **Automation**: Reduces manual effort by calculating, filing, and paying taxes automatically.
- **Accuracy**: Minimizes errors with real-time tax calculations and updates.
- **Compliance**: Keeps you up-to-date with changing tax laws and filing requirements.

- **Time Savings**: Streamlines the entire payroll tax process, freeing up time for other business activities.

Filing state and federal payroll taxes can be complex, but Quick-Books Online makes the process efficient and compliant. By automating calculations, payments, and filings, you can reduce errors, save time, and focus on running your business. With the tools and practices outlined in this chapter, you're well-equipped to handle payroll taxes confidently and ensure your business meets its obligations.

Now that you've mastered tax filing basics, you're ready to explore more advanced QuickBooks Online features. Let's continue to build on this foundation in the next chapter!

CHAPTER 10

INVENTORY AND BUDGETING

Managing inventory and budgeting effectively is critical to maintaining financial stability and meeting customer demands. Inventory and budgeting are interconnected pillars of business success, ensuring that you have the resources to fulfill orders while optimizing costs and achieving financial goals. QuickBooks Online provides powerful tools to streamline these processes, offering real-time insights and automation to simplify decision-making.

In this chapter, we'll explore how to leverage QuickBooks Online for smarter inventory management and budgeting. First, we'll delve into **Tracking Stock Levels**, an essential practice for preventing stockouts and managing the cost of goods sold (COGS). With accurate inventory tracking, you can reduce waste, optimize purchasing decisions, and ensure customer satisfaction.

Next, we'll examine **Creating Budgets**, a critical aspect of financial planning. You'll learn how to set realistic goals, track performance, and adjust budgets dynamically as your business evolves. With QuickBooks Online's budgeting tools, you can align financial resources with your strategic objectives.

Finally, we'll focus on **Low-Stock Alerts**, a proactive feature that ensures you're never caught off guard by inventory shortages. By setting up reminders, you can stay ahead of stock needs, improve cash flow management, and prevent disruptions in your supply chain.

By mastering these techniques, you'll be equipped to balance inventory costs, meet customer demands, and drive your business toward financial success. Let's dive into how QuickBooks Online can simplify inventory and budgeting management for your business!

Tracking Stock Levels: Preventing Stockouts and Managing COGS

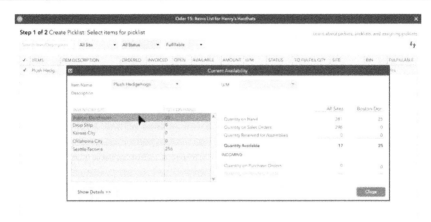

Effective inventory management is vital for businesses that sell products. Tracking stock levels ensures you can meet customer demand without overstocking, which ties up capital and increases storage costs. Additionally, managing the cost of goods sold (COGS) accurately helps you understand profitability and make informed financial decisions. QuickBooks Online provides robust tools to simplify inventory tracking and COGS management, giving you real-time insights and helping you avoid stockouts and overstocking.

In this chapter, we'll explore the importance of tracking stock levels, guide you through using QuickBooks Online for inventory management, and share best practices for preventing stockouts and managing COGS.

1. Why Tracking Stock Levels Matters

Tracking stock levels is more than just counting items in your inventory. It's a strategic practice that directly impacts customer satisfaction, cash flow, and profitability.

1.1. Benefits of Accurate Stock Tracking

- **Customer Satisfaction**: Prevent stockouts and ensure timely order fulfillment.

- **Cost Control**: Avoid overstocking, which leads to excess holding costs and potential obsolescence.
- **Financial Accuracy**: Maintain precise records for financial reporting and tax compliance.
- **Operational Efficiency**: Streamline purchasing decisions and improve supplier relationships.

1.2. Risks of Poor Inventory Management

- Stockouts can lead to lost sales and dissatisfied customers.
- Overstocking ties up cash flow and increases storage costs.
- Inaccurate records can result in errors in financial reporting and tax filings.

2. Understanding Cost of Goods Sold (COGS)

COGS refers to the direct costs of producing or purchasing the goods you sell. Managing COGS is crucial for understanding profitability and setting competitive prices.

2.1. Components of COGS

- **Direct Costs**: Includes the cost of raw materials, labor, and manufacturing.
- **Purchasing Costs**: For retailers, this includes the price of acquiring inventory from suppliers.
- **Shipping and Handling**: Expenses related to transporting inventory.

2.2. Impact on Profitability

- Higher COGS reduces gross profit margins, while effective cost management improves profitability.
- Understanding COGS helps in setting prices that cover costs and maximize margins.

2.3. How QuickBooks Online Tracks COGS

- Automatically calculates COGS based on inventory purchases and sales.
- Generates reports to analyze trends and improve cost efficiency.

3. Using QuickBooks Online to Track Stock Levels

QuickBooks Online simplifies inventory management by providing real-time updates, low-stock alerts, and detailed reports.

3.1. Setting Up Inventory in QuickBooks Online

1. **Enable Inventory Tracking**

- Go to **Settings > Sales** and enable the inventory tracking feature.

2. **Add Inventory Items**

- Navigate to **Sales > Products and Services** and click **New > Inventory**.
- Enter details such as item name, SKU, initial quantity, purchase price, and selling price.

3. **Set Reorder Points**

- Specify minimum stock levels to trigger low-stock alerts.

3.2. Real-Time Inventory Updates

- QuickBooks automatically updates inventory levels when items are sold, purchased, or adjusted.
- Monitor inventory changes in the **Products and Services** dashboard.

3.3. Inventory Reports

1. **Inventory Valuation Summary**

- Provides an overview of total inventory value and quantity.

2. **Inventory Quantity on Hand**

- Lists current stock levels for each item, helping you plan purchases.

3. **COGS Report**

- Displays total COGS over a specified period, allowing you to analyze trends.

4. Preventing Stockouts

Stockouts can harm customer relationships and revenue. QuickBooks Online offers tools to prevent these disruptions.

4.1. Low-Stock Alerts

- Set reorder points for each inventory item. QuickBooks sends notifications when stock levels fall below these thresholds.

4.2. Regular Inventory Audits

- Conduct periodic physical counts to reconcile actual stock with system records.
- Update inventory quantities in QuickBooks Online to maintain accuracy.

4.3. Demand Forecasting

- Use historical sales data to predict future demand and adjust inventory levels accordingly.
- Consider seasonal trends and customer buying patterns.

4.4. Supplier Management

- Build strong relationships with reliable suppliers to ensure timely replenishment.
- Negotiate lead times and minimum order quantities that align with your business needs.

5. Managing Overstocking

While preventing stockouts is essential, overstocking can also strain your resources. Balancing inventory levels is key.

5.1. Identifying Overstocked Items

- Use inventory reports to identify slow-moving or excess stock.
- Analyze sales trends to understand why certain items are overstocked.

5.2. Strategies to Reduce Excess Stock

- **Promotions and Discounts**: Offer discounts or bundle deals to clear out slow-moving items.
- **Liquidation**: Sell excess inventory to clearance buyers or donate it for tax benefits.

5.3. Optimizing Inventory Turnover

- Monitor the inventory turnover ratio to ensure items are sold within a reasonable timeframe.
- Adjust purchasing practices to align with actual sales patterns.

6. Best Practices for Inventory Management

Adopting best practices helps maintain accurate records and optimize stock levels.

6.1. Centralize Inventory Data

- Use QuickBooks Online as the single source of truth for inventory tracking.
- Sync data from sales channels and warehouse systems to avoid duplication.

6.2. Automate Reordering

- Set up automated purchase orders in QuickBooks Online to replenish stock when reorder points are reached.

6.3. Categorize Inventory

- Organize items into categories or classifications to streamline tracking and reporting.

6.4. Monitor Inventory Metrics

- Track key metrics such as:
- Inventory turnover ratio.
- Days sales of inventory (DSI).
- Gross margin return on investment (GMROI).

6.5. Train Staff

- Train employees on proper inventory handling and QuickBooks Online usage to maintain accuracy.

7. Leveraging Advanced Inventory Integrations

For businesses with complex inventory needs, QuickBooks Online integrates with advanced tools such as:

- **TradeGecko (QuickBooks Commerce)**: Tracks inventory across multiple channels and warehouses.
- **Shopify**: Syncs e-commerce sales with QuickBooks to update stock levels in real time.
- **Cin7**: Offers advanced features like batch tracking and demand forecasting.

8. Troubleshooting Inventory Issues

8.1. Discrepancies Between Physical and Recorded Inventory

- **Cause**: Errors in data entry or theft.
- **Solution**: Conduct regular audits and reconcile discrepancies promptly.

8.2. Outdated Stock Records

- **Cause**: Delayed updates from sales channels or warehouses.
- **Solution**: Automate data syncing and ensure timely updates.

8.3. Mismanaged COGS

- **Cause**: Inaccurate purchase records or missing expenses.
- **Solution**: Review purchase orders and ensure all costs are recorded.

9. Benefits of Tracking Stock Levels with QuickBooks Online

By effectively managing stock levels, businesses can achieve:

- **Operational Efficiency**: Streamlined workflows and accurate data reduce manual effort.
- **Cost Savings**: Optimized inventory levels minimize holding costs and waste.
- **Enhanced Customer Satisfaction**: Reliable stock availability improves order fulfillment.
- **Better Decision-Making**: Data-driven insights support strategic planning and financial control.

Tracking stock levels and managing COGS are essential for maintaining a profitable and efficient business. QuickBooks Online provides the tools to monitor inventory in real time, prevent stockouts, and optimize costs. By following the strategies and best practices outlined in this chapter, you can gain greater control over your inventory, enhance customer satisfaction, and drive financial success.

With your inventory under control, you're well-positioned to explore the next step in effective financial management: creating budgets to set and achieve your business goals. Let's continue the journey to mastering QuickBooks Online!

Creating Budgets: Setting Goals and Monitoring Performance

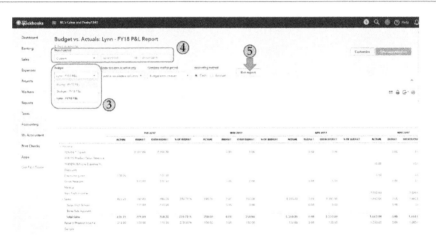

A well-structured budget is a critical tool for business success. It serves as a financial blueprint, helping you allocate resources, set goals, and measure performance over time. Whether you're managing a small business or a growing enterprise, creating and monitoring budgets in QuickBooks Online provides the clarity needed to make informed decisions and achieve your objectives.

In this chapter, we'll explore the importance of budgeting, how to create effective budgets using QuickBooks Online, and strategies for monitoring performance to stay on track. By the end, you'll have the tools and confidence to align your financial plans with your business goals.

1. The Importance of Budgeting

A budget is more than a document; it's a strategic tool that guides your business decisions and ensures financial stability.

1.1. Benefits of Budgeting

- **Financial Clarity**: Understand your revenue, expenses, and cash flow at a glance.
- **Goal Setting**: Define realistic financial goals and prioritize spending.
- **Performance Monitoring**: Compare actual results against budgeted figures to identify variances.
- **Risk Management**: Anticipate financial challenges and adjust plans proactively.

1.2. Common Budgeting Challenges

- Overestimating revenue or underestimating expenses.
- Failing to account for unexpected costs.
- Neglecting to update budgets as conditions change.

2. Types of Budgets

Different types of budgets serve specific purposes depending on your business needs.

2.1. Operating Budget

- Focuses on day-to-day expenses and revenue.
- Covers categories like rent, utilities, payroll, and sales income.

2.2. Cash Flow Budget

- Projects cash inflows and outflows over a specific period.
- Ensures you have sufficient liquidity to cover short-term obligations.

2.3. Capital Budget

- Plans for long-term investments like equipment, technology, or facility upgrades.

2.4. Project-Specific Budget

- Tracks expenses and revenue for individual projects, ensuring profitability.

3. Creating Budgets in QuickBooks Online

QuickBooks Online simplifies the budgeting process, allowing you to create detailed and customizable budgets.

3.1. Setting Up a Budget

1. **Access the Budgeting Tool**
- Navigate to **Settings > Budgeting** in QuickBooks Online.
2. **Create a New Budget**
- Click **Add Budget** and give it a descriptive name, such as "2024 Annual Budget."
3. **Choose the Budget Period**
- Select a time frame (e.g., monthly, quarterly, or yearly).
4. **Select the Budget Type**
- Choose between:
  - **Profit and Loss Budget**: Based on income and expenses.
  - **Project Budget**: Focused on specific projects or departments.

3.2. Inputting Budget Data

1. **Start with Historical Data**
- Use QuickBooks' reports to analyze past performance and guide your projections.
2. **Enter Revenue Projections**
- Estimate income based on sales trends, contracts, or expected growth.
3. **Add Expense Categories**
- Break down expenses into categories like payroll, marketing, and utilities.
4. **Adjust for Seasonal Variations**

- Account for fluctuations in revenue and expenses due to seasonal trends.

3.3. Finalizing the Budget
- Review the budget for accuracy and completeness.
- Save and lock the budget to prevent unauthorized changes.

4. Aligning Budgets with Business Goals
A budget is most effective when aligned with your business objectives.

4.1. Setting SMART Goals
- **Specific**: Clearly define financial targets.
- **Measurable**: Quantify revenue, expense, or profit goals.
- **Achievable**: Set realistic targets based on market conditions.
- **Relevant**: Ensure goals align with your overall business strategy.
- **Time-Bound**: Assign deadlines for achieving each goal.

4.2. Linking Goals to Budget Categories
- Assign specific goals to budget line items. For example:
- Reduce marketing expenses by 10% without impacting lead generation.
- Increase revenue from product sales by 20% in the next quarter.

4.3. Allocating Resources
- Prioritize spending in areas that support your strategic goals, such as new product development or customer acquisition.

5. Monitoring Budget Performance
Monitoring your budget regularly helps you stay on track and make informed adjustments.

5.1. Generating Budget vs. Actual Reports
1. **Access Reports**

- Navigate to **Reports > Budget vs. Actuals** in QuickBooks Online.

2. Analyze Variances

- Compare actual income and expenses to budgeted amounts.
- Highlight variances that require attention.

5.2. Identifying Trends

- Look for patterns in over- or under-spending to refine future budgets.

5.3. Adjusting the Budget

- Update budgeted amounts as conditions change, such as unexpected revenue opportunities or rising costs.

5.4. Regular Reviews

- Schedule monthly or quarterly budget reviews to assess progress and make course corrections.

6. Best Practices for Budgeting

Adopting best practices ensures your budgeting process is effective and efficient.

6.1. Use Realistic Assumptions

- Base projections on historical data, industry benchmarks, and market conditions.

6.2. Involve Key Stakeholders

- Collaborate with team members or departments to create accurate and comprehensive budgets.

6.3. Plan for Contingencies

- Include a contingency fund to cover unexpected expenses or shortfalls.

6.4. Simplify Budget Categories

- Avoid overly detailed budgets that are difficult to manage. Focus on major revenue and expense categories.

6.5. Leverage Automation

- Use QuickBooks Online's budgeting features to automate calculations, track progress, and generate reports.

7. Troubleshooting Common Budgeting Issues

Despite careful planning, challenges may arise during the budgeting process.

7.1. Overestimating Revenue

- **Solution**: Use conservative estimates and consider potential risks.

7.2. Underestimating Expenses

- **Solution**: Review historical spending patterns and account for inflation or rising costs.

7.3. Lack of Alignment with Goals

- **Solution**: Regularly review and update budgets to reflect changing business priorities.

7.4. Poor Tracking

- **Solution**: Use QuickBooks' real-time tracking and reports to monitor progress.

8. The Role of Technology in Budgeting

QuickBooks Online's advanced features enhance your ability to create and manage budgets.

8.1. Real-Time Data

- Access up-to-date financial information to make accurate projections.

8.2. Customizable Reports

- Generate detailed reports tailored to your specific needs.

8.3. Integration with Other Tools

- Sync QuickBooks Online with apps like Excel for advanced data analysis or project management tools for budget tracking.

8.4. Notifications and Alerts

- Set up notifications for budget thresholds or variances to address issues promptly.

9. Benefits of Effective Budgeting

Implementing a structured budgeting process offers significant advantages:

- **Improved Decision-Making**: Make data-driven decisions based on real-time insights.
- **Enhanced Profitability**: Optimize spending and maximize returns.
- **Greater Accountability**: Foster transparency and account- ability across departments.
- **Business Growth**: Align financial resources with strategic initiatives to drive growth.

Creating budgets and monitoring performance are essential practices for achieving financial stability and business success. QuickBooks Online's budgeting tools simplify the process, al- lowing you to set clear goals, allocate resources effectively, and track progress in real time. By following the strategies and best practices outlined in this chapter, you can build a solid financial foundation and adapt to changing conditions with confidence.

With your budgeting process optimized, you're ready to explore additional tools in QuickBooks Online to enhance your financial management. Let's continue on this path to mastering advanced features and achieving your business goals!

Low-Stock Alerts: Configuring Proactive Reminders

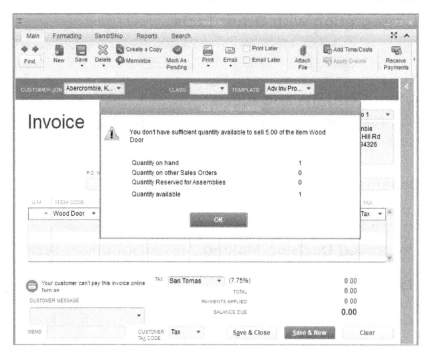

For businesses that manage inventory, maintaining optimal stock levels is essential to avoid costly stockouts or overstocking. Stockouts can lead to missed sales and unhappy customers, while overstocking ties up valuable capital and increases holding costs. Low-stock alerts in QuickBooks Online are a powerful feature that helps businesses stay ahead of inventory needs by providing proactive reminders to reorder items before they run out.

In this chapter, we'll explore the importance of low-stock alerts, guide you through setting them up in QuickBooks Online, and share strategies for using these alerts effectively to maintain a well-balanced inventory.

1. The Importance of Low-Stock Alerts

Low-stock alerts are an essential tool for businesses that sell physical products. They provide a real-time indication of when inventory levels are approaching critical thresholds, enabling timely reordering and ensuring smooth operations.

1.1. Benefits of Low-Stock Alerts

- **Prevent Stockouts**: Reorder items before they run out, maintaining customer satisfaction and sales continuity.
- **Optimize Reordering**: Avoid overstocking by ordering just the right amount of inventory.
- **Save Time**: Automate tracking, reducing the need for manual stock checks.
- **Enhance Cash Flow Management**: Prevent unnecessary capital from being tied up in excess inventory.

1.2. Challenges of Managing Stock Without Alerts

- Frequent manual inventory checks are time-consuming and prone to errors.
- Stockouts disrupt operations, resulting in lost sales and damage to customer relationships.
- Overstocking leads to increased storage costs and the risk of obsolescence.

2. Setting Up Low-Stock Alerts in QuickBooks Online

QuickBooks Online makes it simple to set up low-stock alerts, helping you stay informed about inventory levels in real-time.

2.1. Enabling Inventory Tracking

Before setting up alerts, ensure that inventory tracking is enabled in QuickBooks Online.

1. **Go to Settings**: Navigate to **Settings > Sales** in the QuickBooks menu.
2. **Enable Inventory Tracking**: Check the box for **Track inventory quantity on hand** and save your changes.

2.2. Adding Inventory Items

Low-stock alerts can only be set up for items that are added to your inventory list.

1. **Navigate to Products and Services**: Go to **Sales > Products and Services**.
2. **Create an Inventory Item**:
- Click **New** and select **Inventory**.

- Enter the item name, SKU, and details like cost, sales price, and supplier information.

3. **Set Reorder Points**:

- Specify a minimum quantity (reorder point) for the item. For example, set a reorder point of 10 units if you need to reorder when stock levels fall to 10.

2.3. Activating Low-Stock Alerts

1. **Enable Notifications**: QuickBooks Online automatically generates low-stock alerts for items with defined reorder points.
2. **Monitor Alerts**: Alerts appear in the **Products and Services** dashboard and may also be sent via email, depending on your settings.

3. Using Low-Stock Alerts Effectively

Setting up low-stock alerts is just the first step. To fully leverage this feature, it's important to integrate these alerts into your inventory management strategy.

3.1. Responding to Alerts Promptly

- Act on alerts as soon as they appear to avoid delays in reordering.
- Regularly review the **Products and Services** dashboard for updates on stock levels.

3.2. Establishing Reorder Policies

- Use historical sales data to determine optimal reorder quantities.
- Align reorder points with supplier lead times to prevent stockouts.

3.3. Automating Reorders

QuickBooks Online integrates with third-party apps to streamline reordering.

- **Connect with Suppliers**: Use apps like TradeGecko or Cin7 to automate purchase orders based on low-stock alerts.

- **Create Recurring Purchase Orders**: Set up recurring orders for high-demand items with consistent usage.

3.4. Analyzing Stock Trends

- Use reports like **Inventory Quantity on Hand** and **Sales by Product/Service** to identify trends and adjust reorder points as needed.

4. Configuring Alerts for Different Business Needs

Every business has unique inventory requirements. Tailor your low-stock alerts to meet specific needs.

4.1. Seasonal Adjustments

- Modify reorder points during peak seasons to account for increased demand.
- Reduce reorder points during slow periods to prevent over-stocking.

4.2. High-Value Items

- Set tighter reorder thresholds for high-value items or products critical to your operations.

4.3. Perishable Inventory

- For businesses handling perishable goods, configure alerts to ensure items are used or sold before expiration.

4.4. Multi-Location Tracking

- If you manage inventory across multiple locations, use Quick-Books integrations to monitor stock levels at each site and configure location-specific reorder points.

5. Leveraging Reports to Support Low-Stock Alerts

QuickBooks Online's reporting tools complement low-stock alerts by providing deeper insights into inventory performance.

5.1. Inventory Valuation Summary

- Understand the total value of your inventory on hand, including quantities and costs.

5.2. Inventory Quantity on Hand

- Identify which items are nearing their reorder points and prioritize reorders accordingly.

5.3. Sales by Product/Service

- Analyze sales trends to adjust reorder points and quantities based on demand patterns.

5.4. Inventory Turnover Ratio

- Monitor how quickly inventory is sold and replaced to optimize stock levels.

6. Best Practices for Using Low-Stock Alerts

Adopting best practices ensures that low-stock alerts contribute effectively to your inventory management strategy.

6.1. Regularly Review Reorder Points

- Reassess reorder points periodically to reflect changes in demand or supplier lead times.

6.2. Combine Alerts with Demand Forecasting

- Use sales and market data to predict future demand and set proactive reorder points.

6.3. Train Employees

- Ensure team members responsible for inventory understand how to use low-stock alerts and respond promptly.

6.4. Integrate with Other Systems

- Sync QuickBooks Online with inventory management tools for a seamless workflow.

6.5. Audit Inventory Regularly

- Conduct physical inventory counts to verify that actual stock matches system records and adjust as necessary.

7. Troubleshooting Common Issues with Low-Stock Alerts

While low-stock alerts are highly effective, occasional issues may arise. Here's how to address them:

7.1. Missing Alerts

- **Cause**: Reorder points not set for certain items.
- **Solution**: Review the **Products and Services** list and define reorder points for all inventory items.

7.2. Incorrect Alerts

- **Cause**: Errors in recorded stock levels.
- **Solution**: Conduct a physical count and reconcile discrepancies in QuickBooks Online.

7.3. Delayed Notifications

- **Cause**: Alerts not checked regularly.
- **Solution**: Enable email notifications or set reminders to review the dashboard frequently.

8. Benefits of Low-Stock Alerts

Low-stock alerts offer significant advantages for businesses of all sizes:

- **Efficiency**: Automates stock tracking and reduces manual effort.
- **Accuracy**: Ensures timely reorders and maintains optimal inventory levels.
- **Cost Savings**: Prevents overstocking and minimizes carrying costs.
- **Customer Satisfaction**: Improves order fulfillment and avoids delays caused by stockouts.

Low-stock alerts are a powerful feature that helps businesses maintain optimal inventory levels and prevent costly disruptions. By configuring proactive reminders in QuickBooks Online, you can stay ahead of inventory needs, respond promptly to changing demands, and make informed decisions about reordering. Combined with robust inventory management practices, low-stock alerts ensure your business operates efficiently and profitably.

With your inventory management system enhanced by low-stock alerts, you're ready to explore other advanced features in QuickBooks Online to further streamline your operations. Let's continue optimizing your financial management tools!

CHAPTER 11
ADVANCED REPORTING AND ANALYTICS

In today's data-driven world, having access to tailored insights is essential for making informed business decisions. QuickBooks Online offers powerful reporting and analytics tools that allow you to dive deep into your financial data, helping you uncover opportunities, address challenges, and plan strategically for growth. Advanced reporting features transform raw numbers into actionable insights, making it easier to steer your business toward success.

This chapter will guide you through three critical aspects of advanced reporting and analytics. First, we'll explore **Customizing Reports**, a feature that allows you to tailor reports to your business's specific needs. By focusing on the data that matters most, you can gain clear insights into your financial health, sales performance, and expense trends.

Next, we'll discuss **Forecasting Growth** using financial data. With QuickBooks Online's forecasting tools, you'll learn how to identify trends, predict future revenue and expenses, and make strategic decisions to support sustainable growth.

Finally, we'll cover **Audit Logs**, a crucial feature for ensuring data integrity and maintaining a reliable record of all changes made in your QuickBooks account. Audit logs help you track modifications, prevent fraud, and ensure compliance with legal and regulatory standards.

By mastering these advanced reporting and analytics features, you'll gain the confidence and clarity needed to make data-driven decisions and take your business to the next level. Let's explore how QuickBooks Online's reporting tools can empower your success!

Customizing Reports: Tailored Insights for Your Business

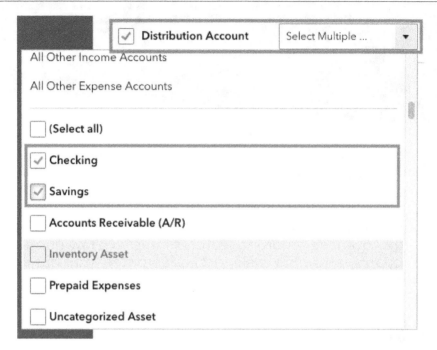

In the world of business, data is power. However, raw data is often overwhelming without the tools to make it meaningful. Quick-Books Online offers a suite of customizable reporting features that allow you to extract, organize, and analyze the financial information that matters most to your business. Custom reports transform your financial data into actionable insights, enabling you to make smarter decisions, identify trends, and plan strategically.

In this chapter, we'll explore the importance of customizing reports, guide you through the process of tailoring reports in Quick-Books Online, and provide practical tips for leveraging these insights to improve your business performance.

1. Why Custom Reports Are Important

Standard financial reports provide a broad overview of your business, but they may not address your unique needs. Customizing reports allows you to focus on the specific data points and metrics that are most relevant to your goals.

1.1. Benefits of Custom Reports

- **Focus on What Matters**: Highlight key metrics, such as profitability, cash flow, or customer spending habits.
- **Save Time**: Automate recurring custom reports to avoid repetitive data extraction.
- **Enhanced Decision-Making**: Use tailored insights to guide your business strategy.
- **Increased Accuracy**: Eliminate irrelevant data that could distract or confuse stakeholders.

1.2. Common Use Cases

- **Budget Tracking**: Compare actual performance against budgeted figures.
- **Profitability Analysis**: Identify your most profitable products or services.
- **Customer Insights**: Track spending patterns and evaluate customer value.
- **Expense Monitoring**: Highlight areas where costs can be reduced.

2. How to Customize Reports in QuickBooks Online

QuickBooks Online provides an intuitive interface for creating and customizing reports to suit your needs.

2.1. Accessing the Reports Center

1. Navigate to the **Reports** menu on the left-hand navigation panel.
2. Browse the categories, such as "Business Overview," "Sales," or "Expenses," to find a base report that aligns with your goals.

2.2. Selecting a Base Report

Choose a standard report to start with, such as:

- **Profit and Loss Statement**: Tracks income and expenses over a period.

- **Balance Sheet**: Provides a snapshot of your assets, liabilities, and equity.
- **Sales by Customer Summary**: Highlights revenue generated by each customer.

2.3. Customizing the Report

QuickBooks Online allows you to customize reports by adjusting filters, data ranges, and formatting.

1.   Adjust Filters

- Use filters to include or exclude specific data, such as:
  - Customers.
  - Products or services.
  - Payment methods.
  - Locations or classes.

2.   Change Date Ranges

- Set custom date ranges to analyze specific time periods (e.g., monthly, quarterly, annually).

3.   Modify Columns and Rows

- Add, remove, or rearrange columns to focus on relevant data points.
- Examples: Add a column for tax details or a row for product categories.

4.   Group Data

- Organize data into groups, such as by customer, project, or sales region, to identify trends.

5.   Apply Formatting

- Adjust font size, color, or report layout for easier readability and presentation.

2.4. Saving and Automating Reports

1.   Save the Custom Report

- Click **Save Customization** to preserve your changes.

2.   Create a Custom Report Group

- Organize saved reports into groups for easy access.

3.   Automate Reports

- Set up recurring reports to be generated and emailed automatically at specified intervals.

3. Types of Custom Reports for Your Business

Different businesses have unique reporting needs. Here are examples of how custom reports can provide value:

3.1. Small Retail Businesses

- **Inventory Reports**: Track stock levels and monitor top-selling items.
- **Sales by Product/Service**: Identify which products drive the most revenue.

3.2. Service-Based Businesses

- **Profitability by Project**: Evaluate which projects or clients are most profitable.
- **Time Tracking Reports**: Analyze billable hours by employee or service.

3.3. E-Commerce Businesses

- **Sales by Channel**: Compare revenue from different platforms, such as Shopify or Amazon.
- **Customer Retention Reports**: Monitor repeat customers and average purchase values.

3.4. Nonprofits

- **Donor Contribution Reports**: Track donations by individual or organization.
- **Grant Reports**: Analyze how grant funds are allocated and spent.

4. Advanced Customization Features

For businesses with more complex needs, QuickBooks Online offers advanced customization options.

4.1. Custom Fields

- Add custom fields to track unique data points, such as:

- Purchase order numbers.
- Project codes.
- Customer preferences.

4.2. Classes and Locations

- Use classes to categorize transactions by department, project, or type of work.
- Use locations to analyze data across different store locations or service areas.

4.3. Comparative Reports

- Create side-by-side comparisons of performance across different periods, customers, or product categories.

4.4. Exporting Data

- Export reports to Excel or Google Sheets for additional analysis or integration with other tools.

5. Best Practices for Customizing Reports

To maximize the value of your custom reports, follow these best practices:

5.1. Define Clear Objectives

- Before creating a report, identify the questions you want to answer or the insights you need.

5.2. Keep Reports Focused

- Avoid cluttering reports with too much data. Focus on the metrics that directly impact your decisions.

5.3. Update Regularly

- Refresh reports with the latest data to ensure accuracy and relevance.

5.4. Collaborate with Stakeholders

- Share custom reports with team members or stakeholders to ensure alignment on goals and priorities.

5.5. Use Visual Aids

- Incorporate charts, graphs, and tables to make data more accessible and visually appealing.

6. Troubleshooting Common Reporting Issues

While QuickBooks Online makes customization easy, occasional challenges may arise. Here's how to address them:

6.1. Missing Data

- **Cause**: Filters may exclude relevant data.
- **Solution**: Review and adjust filters to ensure all necessary data is included.

6.2. Incorrect Formatting

- **Cause**: Columns or rows are misplaced or contain redundant information.
- **Solution**: Modify layout settings to create a clearer structure.

6.3. Inconsistent Metrics

- **Cause**: Custom fields or categories are not standardized.
- **Solution**: Establish consistent naming conventions for categories and custom fields.

6.4. Difficulty Sharing Reports

- **Cause**: Recipients lack access to QuickBooks Online.
- **Solution**: Export reports as PDFs or Excel files for easy distribution.

7. Leveraging Reports for Strategic Insights

Custom reports are only valuable if you use them to drive decisions. Here are ways to apply insights from your reports:

7.1. Identify Growth Opportunities

- Use sales reports to identify high-performing products, services, or customers.

7.2. Control Costs

- Analyze expense reports to find areas for cost reduction or optimization.

7.3. Monitor Cash Flow

- Use cash flow reports to ensure sufficient liquidity for operations and investments.

7.4. Align with Goals

- Regularly review budget vs. actual reports to measure progress toward financial goals.

8. Benefits of Custom Reports in QuickBooks Online

Customizing reports in QuickBooks Online offers numerous benefits:

- **Efficiency**: Save time with automated, recurring reports tailored to your needs.
- **Accuracy**: Focus on relevant data, reducing the risk of misinterpretation.
- **Scalability**: Adjust reports as your business grows or priorities change.
- **Transparency**: Share clear, actionable insights with your team or stakeholders.

Customizing reports in QuickBooks Online empowers you to transform data into actionable insights. By tailoring reports to your unique business needs, you can focus on what matters most, improve decision-making, and monitor performance effectively. Whether you're tracking profitability, analyzing customer behavior, or controlling expenses, custom reports provide the clarity and precision needed to drive success.

With a firm grasp of customized reporting, you're ready to delve into using these insights for strategic planning and growth forecasting. Let's continue exploring how QuickBooks Online's advanced features can elevate your financial management!

Forecasting Growth: Using Financial Data for Strategic Planning

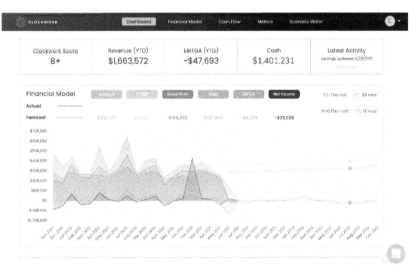

Forecasting growth is an essential aspect of strategic planning for any business. By leveraging financial data, you can predict future trends, set realistic goals, and prepare for challenges. Growth forecasting isn't just about estimating revenue—it's about understanding how various factors, such as market trends, operating expenses, and customer behavior, interact to shape your business's future.

QuickBooks Online offers powerful tools and insights that simplify growth forecasting by providing access to real-time financial data and advanced reporting features. In this chapter, we'll explore the importance of forecasting growth, guide you through using financial data effectively, and share strategies for integrating forecasts into your strategic planning process.

1. Why Forecasting Growth Is Crucial

Forecasting growth is a forward-looking exercise that aligns your business goals with actionable insights derived from historical data.

1.1. Benefits of Growth Forecasting

- **Informed Decision-Making**: Make data-driven decisions about investments, staffing, and inventory management.
- **Goal Setting**: Define achievable targets for revenue, expenses, and profitability.
- **Risk Mitigation**: Identify potential challenges and prepare contingency plans.
- **Resource Allocation**: Optimize resource allocation for marketing, operations, and product development.

1.2. Challenges of Growth Forecasting

- Uncertain market conditions and economic fluctuations can impact projections.
- Limited historical data for new businesses may make forecasting more complex.
- Over-optimistic forecasts can lead to poor decision-making and overinvestment.

2. Key Components of Growth Forecasting

Accurate forecasting relies on analyzing various components of your financial data.

2.1. Revenue Trends

- **Historical Revenue**: Review past revenue trends to identify growth patterns.
- **Revenue Drivers**: Understand what drives revenue, such as product sales, service contracts, or recurring subscriptions.

2.2. Expense Trends

- **Fixed Costs**: Monitor consistent expenses like rent and salaries.
- **Variable Costs**: Analyze costs that fluctuate with sales volume, such as raw materials or shipping.

2.3. Customer Behavior

- **Customer Acquisition**: Track how many new customers you gain over time.
- **Customer Retention**: Evaluate repeat business and customer loyalty metrics.

- **Average Transaction Value (ATV)**: Monitor the average value of customer purchases.

2.4. Market Trends

- **Industry Benchmarks**: Compare your business performance against industry standards.
- **Seasonal Trends**: Identify periods of increased or decreased demand.

3. Leveraging QuickBooks Online for Growth Forecasting

QuickBooks Online provides a wealth of financial data and reporting tools to support growth forecasting.

3.1. Using Historical Data

1. **Access Reports**: Navigate to the **Reports** section in QuickBooks Online to generate financial statements.
2. **Review Trends**:

- **Profit and Loss (P&L) Statement**: Analyze revenue, expenses, and profitability over time.
- **Sales by Product/Service**: Identify top-performing products or services.
- **Cash Flow Statement**: Track cash inflows and outflows to ensure liquidity.

3.2. Creating Projections

1. **Set a Time Frame**:

- Choose a forecast period, such as monthly, quarterly, or yearly.

2. **Estimate Revenue Growth**:

- Base projections on historical growth rates and expected market conditions.

3. **Estimate Expenses**:

- Break down expenses into fixed and variable categories, projecting changes based on anticipated growth.

3.3. Generating Comparative Reports

- Use the **Budget vs. Actual** report to compare forecasted figures with actual results, identifying variances and refining forecasts.

3.4. Customizing Reports

- Create custom reports to focus on specific metrics, such as customer acquisition costs (CAC) or gross margin trends.

4. Strategies for Accurate Growth Forecasting

4.1. Use Multiple Scenarios

- Create optimistic, realistic, and pessimistic forecasts to account for varying market conditions.

4.2. Factor in Market Research

- Incorporate external data, such as industry reports or economic indicators, to validate your assumptions.

4.3. Monitor Key Performance Indicators (KPIs)

- Identify KPIs relevant to your growth strategy, such as:
- Revenue growth rate.
- Gross profit margin.
- Customer lifetime value (CLV).
- Operating expense ratio.

4.4. Integrate Technology

- Leverage tools like QuickBooks Online integrations with CRM or e-commerce platforms to consolidate data and improve accuracy.

5. Integrating Growth Forecasts into Strategic Planning

Growth forecasts are most valuable when they inform actionable strategies.

5.1. Align Forecasts with Business Goals

- Use forecasts to set SMART (Specific, Measurable, Achievable, Relevant, Time-Bound) goals.
- Example: Increase revenue by 15% over the next quarter by expanding your customer base and increasing the average transaction value.

5.2. Resource Planning

- Allocate resources effectively based on forecasted needs, such as hiring additional staff, increasing inventory, or investing in marketing campaigns.

5.3. Financial Planning

- Ensure sufficient cash flow to support growth initiatives by integrating forecasts into your budgeting process.

5.4. Risk Management

- Use pessimistic scenarios to prepare contingency plans, such as reducing discretionary spending or securing additional financing.

6. Common Growth Forecasting Mistakes and How to Avoid Them

6.1. Overreliance on Historical Data

- **Mistake**: Assuming past trends will continue unchanged.
- **Solution**: Factor in current market conditions and future risks.

6.2. Ignoring External Factors

- **Mistake**: Neglecting industry trends, economic conditions, or competitive dynamics.
- **Solution**: Conduct regular market research to supplement internal data.

6.3. Inadequate Scenario Planning

- **Mistake**: Relying on a single growth projection.

- **Solution**: Create multiple scenarios to account for uncertainties.

6.4. Failure to Update Forecasts

- **Mistake**: Using outdated forecasts that don't reflect recent performance or changes.
- **Solution**: Regularly review and update forecasts to stay aligned with current conditions.

7. Advanced Forecasting Techniques

For businesses with complex growth goals, advanced forecasting techniques provide deeper insights.

7.1. Rolling Forecasts

- Continuously update forecasts to reflect the most recent financial and operational data.

7.2. Break-Even Analysis

- Determine the sales volume required to cover costs and achieve profitability.

7.3. Trend Analysis

- Use historical data to identify long-term growth patterns and anticipate future trends.

7.4. Machine Learning and AI Tools

- Integrate predictive analytics tools to improve the accuracy of your forecasts.

8. Benefits of Growth Forecasting with QuickBooks Online

Using QuickBooks Online for growth forecasting provides several advantages:

- **Efficiency**: Automate data collection and calculations to save time.
- **Accuracy**: Leverage real-time data for precise forecasts.

- **Scalability**: Adjust forecasts easily as your business grows or conditions change.
- **Insights**: Gain actionable insights that align with your strategic objectives.

Forecasting growth using financial data is a cornerstone of effective strategic planning. By leveraging QuickBooks Online's tools and insights, you can create accurate projections, set meaningful goals, and prepare your business for a successful future. Whether you're planning for short-term milestones or long-term growth, forecasting provides the clarity and confidence needed to navigate challenges and seize opportunities.

Armed with the knowledge and strategies outlined in this chapter, you're ready to integrate growth forecasts into your overall business strategy, paving the way for sustainable success. Let's continue exploring how QuickBooks Online's advanced features can elevate your business planning and financial management!

Audit Logs: Ensuring Data Integrity

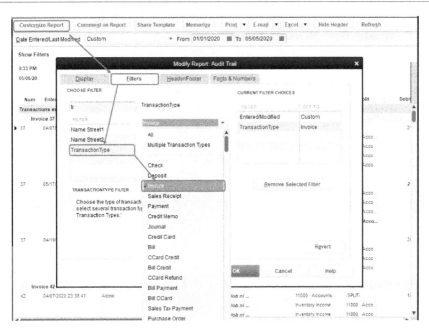

Maintaining data integrity is essential for effective financial management, compliance, and trust within your business. When multiple users interact with your QuickBooks Online account, tracking changes to financial records is crucial. Audit logs are a powerful feature in QuickBooks Online that provide a detailed record of every action taken within your account. These logs offer transparency, help resolve discrepancies, and ensure that your financial data remains accurate and reliable.

In this chapter, we'll explore the importance of audit logs, guide you through accessing and interpreting them in QuickBooks Online, and discuss best practices for using them to ensure data integrity and compliance.

1. Why Audit Logs Matter

Audit logs are more than just a tool for tracking changes; they are a safeguard for your financial data and business operations.

1.1. Benefits of Audit Logs

- **Data Integrity**: Ensure that your financial records are accurate and consistent.
- **Transparency**: Track who made changes, what was modified, and when the action occurred.
- **Dispute Resolution**: Resolve discrepancies quickly by identifying the source of errors or changes.
- **Compliance**: Maintain audit-ready records for tax authorities, regulators, or stakeholders.
- **Fraud Prevention**: Detect unauthorized changes or suspicious activity.

1.2. Risks Without Audit Logs

- Inaccurate financial records due to untracked changes.
- Increased vulnerability to fraud or unauthorized access.
- Difficulty identifying and resolving errors during audits or reconciliations.

2. Accessing the Audit Log in QuickBooks Online

QuickBooks Online makes it easy to access and use audit logs to track changes and ensure data integrity.

2.1. Navigating to the Audit Log

1. **Log in to QuickBooks Online**: Use an administrator account for full access.
2. **Access the Gear Icon**: Click the gear icon in the top-right corner of the dashboard.
3. **Select Audit Log**: Under the "Tools" section, choose **Audit Log**.

2.2. Viewing the Audit Log

1. **Filter and Search**:
- Use filters to narrow down results by date range, user, or event type (e.g., invoices, transactions, settings).
2. **Review the Log**:
- Each entry includes:
    □ **Date and Time**: When the action occurred.
    □ **User**: Who performed the action.
    □ **Event**: What was changed or modified.
    □ **Details**: A description of the action taken, such as "Invoice created" or "Customer details updated."

2.3. Exporting the Audit Log

- Export the audit log to Excel or PDF for offline analysis or sharing with auditors or stakeholders.

3. Using Audit Logs to Ensure Data Integrity

Audit logs provide valuable insights that help you maintain accurate and reliable financial records.

3.1. Tracking User Activity

- Monitor the actions of individual users to ensure they are operating within their roles and responsibilities.
- Example: Confirm that only authorized users are creating or modifying payroll data.

3.2. Identifying and Resolving Errors

- Audit logs help trace errors back to their source, allowing you to correct discrepancies promptly.
- Example: If a bank transaction is miscategorized, the log will show who made the change and when.

3.3. Monitoring Changes to Settings

- Review changes to system settings, such as tax codes, account configurations, or permissions, to ensure they align with your policies.

3.4. Supporting Reconciliations

- Use the audit log to verify adjustments made during bank or credit card reconciliations.

4. Leveraging Audit Logs for Compliance

Audit logs play a critical role in meeting regulatory and tax compliance requirements.

4.1. Preparing for Audits

- Provide detailed records of all changes to financial data, demonstrating that your books are accurate and well-maintained.
- Example: During a tax audit, use the audit log to show when and why specific transactions were adjusted.

4.2. Ensuring Role-Based Access

- Verify that users are accessing only the areas of QuickBooks Online relevant to their role.
- Example: Ensure that sensitive financial data is accessible only to authorized personnel, such as accountants or administrators.

4.3. Meeting Industry Standards

- Some industries, such as finance or healthcare, require detailed change logs to comply with data security and record-keeping standards.

5. Best Practices for Using Audit Logs

Maximize the effectiveness of audit logs by incorporating these best practices into your data management processes.

5.1. Regularly Review the Audit Log

- Schedule periodic reviews of the audit log to identify unusual or unauthorized activity.

5.2. Train Users

- Educate team members on the importance of accurate data entry and the role of audit logs in maintaining integrity.

5.3. Use Role-Based Permissions

- Assign appropriate access levels to users to minimize the risk of unauthorized changes.

5.4. Integrate Logs with Security Protocols

- Combine audit log reviews with other security measures, such as two-factor authentication, to enhance data protection.

5.5. Maintain Backup Records

- Keep regular backups of your financial data and audit logs to protect against accidental deletions or cyber threats.

6. Troubleshooting Common Audit Log Issues

While audit logs are straightforward, you may encounter occasional challenges. Here's how to resolve them:

6.1. Missing Entries

- **Cause**: Filters may exclude certain results.
- **Solution**: Adjust filters to broaden your search parameters.

6.2. Unauthorized Changes

- **Cause**: A user with inappropriate access levels made changes.
- **Solution**: Restrict access permissions and review the log to identify and reverse unauthorized actions.

6.3. Difficulty Interpreting Logs

- **Cause**: Complex or unclear event descriptions.
- **Solution**: Consult QuickBooks support or your accountant for clarification.

7. Integrating Audit Logs with Broader Business Processes

Audit logs are most effective when integrated into your broader business and financial management workflows.

7.1. Risk Management

- Use logs to monitor for anomalies or irregularities that could indicate fraud or errors.

7.2. Team Accountability

- Review logs during performance evaluations or team meetings to highlight adherence to processes.

7.3. Continuous Improvement

- Identify patterns in errors or changes to improve processes and training.

7.4. Collaborating with Auditors

- Share audit logs with external auditors to streamline compliance checks and reporting.

8. Benefits of Using Audit Logs

Audit logs offer significant advantages for businesses of all sizes:

- **Transparency**: Enhance trust within your team and with stakeholders by maintaining clear records of all changes.
- **Efficiency**: Resolve errors or discrepancies quickly, minimizing downtime.
- **Compliance**: Simplify audits and ensure adherence to legal and regulatory requirements.
- **Security**: Detect and address unauthorized actions promptly, reducing the risk of fraud.

Audit logs are an invaluable feature of QuickBooks Online, providing a comprehensive record of all changes made within your account. By leveraging audit logs, you can ensure data integrity, enhance transparency, and maintain compliance with confidence. Whether you're tracking user activity, resolving errors, or preparing for an audit, these logs give you the insights needed to protect and optimize your financial operations.

With a strong understanding of audit logs, you're equipped to build a secure and reliable financial management system. Let's continue exploring other advanced QuickBooks Online features to further strengthen your business's financial foundation!

CHAPTER 12
TROUBLESHOOTING AND EFFICIENCY HACKS

Running a business comes with its fair share of challenges, and managing finances is no exception. Whether you're dealing with unexpected technical glitches, navigating syncing issues, or seeking ways to streamline your workflow, having the right tools and strategies at your disposal is essential. This chapter focuses on practical solutions to common QuickBooks Online challenges and efficiency hacks to help you work smarter, not harder.

First, we'll address **Common Errors and Fixes**, such as login problems, syncing issues, and data discrepancies. By understanding how to diagnose and resolve these issues, you can minimize disruptions and maintain smooth operations.

Next, we'll introduce **Keyboard Shortcuts** that can dramatically speed up your daily workflow. These time-saving hacks allow you to navigate QuickBooks Online more efficiently, reducing the effort required to complete routine tasks.

Finally, we'll explore **Best Practices for Organized Bookkeeping**, offering tips to keep your financial records accurate, consistent, and audit-ready. From regular reconciliations to leveraging automation, these practices ensure that your books remain a reliable foundation for decision-making and compliance.

By mastering these troubleshooting techniques and efficiency strategies, you'll be better equipped to handle the complexities of financial management with ease and confidence. Let's dive in and discover how QuickBooks Online can become an even more powerful tool for your business!

Common Errors and Fixes: Addressing Login and Syncing Issues

QuickBooks Online is a powerful tool for managing your business finances, but like any software, it can occasionally present challenges. Login problems and syncing issues are two of the most common hurdles users face. While these issues can be frustrating, they are usually straightforward to resolve with the right steps.

This chapter provides a detailed guide to diagnosing and fixing common login and syncing problems in QuickBooks Online. By understanding the causes and solutions for these issues, you can minimize disruptions and keep your financial operations running smoothly.

1. Common Login Issues in QuickBooks Online

Logging into QuickBooks Online is a routine task, but various factors can sometimes prevent access. Here are the most common login problems and their solutions.

1.1. Incorrect Login Credentials

- **Problem**: Users often mistype their email address or password.
- **Solution**:
    1. Double-check your login credentials for accuracy.
    2. Use the "Show Password" option (if available) to verify the password you are entering.
    3. Reset your password by clicking the **"Forgot Password"** link and following the prompts.

1.2. Browser Compatibility Issues

- **Problem**: QuickBooks Online may not work correctly with outdated browsers.
- **Solution**:
    1. Ensure you are using a supported browser, such as Google Chrome, Mozilla Firefox, Microsoft Edge, or Safari.
    2. Update your browser to the latest version.
    3. Clear your browser's cache and cookies:
    - ☐ Access your browser's settings.
    - ☐ Locate the cache and cookie settings and clear them.
    - ☐ Restart your browser and attempt to log in again.

1.3. Account Locked

- **Problem**: Multiple failed login attempts can lock your account.
- **Solution**:
    1. Wait for at least 15 minutes and try again.
    2. If the account remains locked, reset your password or contact QuickBooks Online support.

1.4. Two-Factor Authentication Issues

- **Problem**: Delayed or missing verification codes can prevent login.
- **Solution**:
    1. Ensure your registered email or phone number is active and accessible.
    2. Check your spam folder for missing emails.
    3. Update your contact information if it is outdated.

1.5. Network Connectivity Problems

- **Problem**: Poor or unstable internet connections can disrupt the login process.
- **Solution**:
    1. Test your internet speed and ensure a stable connection.
    2. Switch to a different network or use a wired connection if necessary.

2. Common Syncing Issues in QuickBooks Online

Syncing issues occur when data does not transfer correctly between QuickBooks Online and integrated apps or services, such as bank accounts, payment processors, or inventory management tools. These problems can lead to data discrepancies and operational delays.

2.1. Bank Syncing Errors

- **Problem**: Bank transactions fail to sync or appear incorrectly in QuickBooks Online.
- **Solution**:
  1. **Verify Bank Connection**:
     - Go to **Banking > Banking Tab** and check the status of the connected account.
  2. **Update Bank Feeds**:
     - Click **Update** in the Banking tab to refresh the connection and pull in recent transactions.
  3. **Reauthorize Bank Access**:
     - Some banks require periodic reauthorization for security purposes. Follow prompts to reconnect.
  4. **Exclude Duplicate Transactions**:
     - Review the Banking tab for duplicates and exclude them from your records.

2.2. Payment Processor Sync Issues

- **Problem**: Payment data from apps like PayPal, Stripe, or Square does not appear correctly in QuickBooks Online.
- **Solution**:
  1. **Check App Settings**:
     - Ensure that the integration between QuickBooks and the payment processor is active and configured correctly.
  2. **Resync Transactions**:
     - Manually trigger a sync within the payment app or QuickBooks.
  3. **Resolve Mapping Errors**:

- ☐ Map payment categories (e.g., fees, refunds) accurately within QuickBooks to avoid mismatches.

2.3. Inventory Sync Problems

- **Problem**: Inventory levels in QuickBooks Online do not match those in integrated inventory management apps.
- **Solution**:

  1. **Reconcile Inventory Records**:
  - ☐ Compare records in QuickBooks and the inventory app to identify discrepancies.

  2. **Adjust Inventory Quantities**:
  - ☐ Use QuickBooks' **Inventory Adjustment** feature to correct inaccuracies.

  3. **Ensure Compatibility**:
  - ☐ Confirm that the third-party app supports full integration with QuickBooks Online.

2.4. Data Mapping Issues

- **Problem**: Incorrect data mapping causes mismatches during syncing.
- **Solution**:

  1. **Review Mapping Settings**:
  - ☐ Check how data fields (e.g., customer names, categories) are mapped between QuickBooks and the external app.

  2. **Update Mapping Rules**:
  - ☐ Adjust mappings to ensure data flows correctly between systems.

2.5. Duplicate or Missing Transactions

- **Problem**: Synced data includes duplicates or omits certain entries.
- **Solution**:

  1. **Check Sync Logs**:
  - ☐ Review sync logs in QuickBooks or the integrated app to identify errors.

2. **Manually Add Missing Data**:
   ☐ Enter missing transactions directly into QuickBooks.
3. **Exclude Duplicates**:
   ☐ Use the **Exclude** option in the Banking tab to remove duplicate entries.

3. General Troubleshooting Tips

For both login and syncing issues, these general troubleshooting steps can often resolve problems:

3.1. Restart Your Device

- A simple restart can clear temporary glitches affecting Quick-Books Online functionality.

3.2. Update Software

- Ensure QuickBooks Online, your browser, and any integrated apps are updated to their latest versions.

3.3. Disable Browser Extensions

- Extensions, such as ad blockers or VPNs, can interfere with QuickBooks functionality. Disable them temporarily and try again.

3.4. Clear Cache and Cookies

- Accumulated cache or cookies can cause unexpected behavior. Clear these periodically to maintain performance.

3.5. Check for Service Outages

- Visit QuickBooks Online's **Status Page** to verify if there are ongoing outages or maintenance periods.

3.6. Contact Support

- If issues persist, reach out to QuickBooks Online customer support for assistance.

4. Best Practices to Prevent Issues

4.1. Maintain Secure Login Practices

- Use strong passwords and enable two-factor authentication for added security.
- Avoid sharing login credentials with unauthorized users.

4.2. Regularly Review Connections

- Periodically check the status of connected bank accounts, payment processors, and other integrations to ensure they remain active.

4.3. Schedule Syncing

- Schedule syncing during low-traffic times to reduce the risk of interruptions.

4.4. Monitor User Activity

- Use the **Audit Log** in QuickBooks Online to track user activity and detect unauthorized changes.

4.5. Backup Data

- Regularly export key data to create a secure backup of your financial records.

5. When to Seek Professional Assistance

Sometimes, resolving login or syncing issues requires professional help. Contact QuickBooks support or consult an accountant if:

- Syncing errors cause significant discrepancies in financial records.
- You encounter persistent login issues despite troubleshooting.
- You need assistance with complex integrations or data recovery.

While login and syncing issues can be disruptive, QuickBooks Online provides the tools and resources needed to address them effectively. By understanding common problems and their solutions, you can ensure smooth operations and maintain the integrity of your financial data. Equipped with the troubleshooting tips and best practices outlined in this chapter, you're well-prepared to tackle any challenges that arise and continue managing your finances with confidence.

Let's explore how efficiency hacks and best practices can further optimize your workflow in the next section!

Keyboard Shortcuts: Accelerating Your Daily Workflow

Efficiency is a cornerstone of effective financial management, and in QuickBooks Online, every second saved can be used to focus on more strategic tasks. Keyboard shortcuts are a powerful way to streamline your daily workflow, allowing you to navigate the platform, perform routine tasks, and access essential features quickly and effortlessly.

In this chapter, we'll explore the value of keyboard shortcuts, provide a comprehensive list of shortcuts available in QuickBooks Online, and share tips for incorporating them into your daily workflow. By mastering these shortcuts, you can significantly boost your productivity and enhance your overall QuickBooks experience.

1. Why Use Keyboard Shortcuts?

Keyboard shortcuts are designed to save time by minimizing the need for mouse clicks and menu navigation. They are particularly beneficial for users who regularly perform repetitive tasks in QuickBooks Online.

1.1. Benefits of Keyboard Shortcuts

- **Speed**: Perform actions faster than navigating through menus.
- **Efficiency**: Reduce the cognitive load by simplifying navigation and task execution.
- **Precision**: Avoid accidental clicks or selections by using direct commands.
- **Productivity**: Complete tasks quickly, leaving more time for analysis and decision-making.

1.2. Common Scenarios Where Shortcuts Help

- Creating new transactions, such as invoices or expenses.
- Navigating between sections like banking, sales, or reports.
- Generating and customizing financial reports.
- Accessing frequently used tools or features.

2. Essential QuickBooks Online Keyboard Shortcuts

QuickBooks Online offers a variety of keyboard shortcuts that cover navigation, data entry, and specific commands.

2.1. General Navigation Shortcuts

These shortcuts help you move between key areas of QuickBooks Online:

- **Alt + H**: Open the help menu.
- **Ctrl + Alt +?**: Display the list of available keyboard shortcuts.
- **Ctrl + Alt + I**: Create a new invoice.
- **Ctrl + Alt + E**: Record a new expense.
- **Ctrl + Alt + J**: Open the journal entry window.
- **Ctrl + Alt + A**: Open the chart of accounts.
- **Ctrl + Alt + R**: Access reports.

2.2. Transaction-Specific Shortcuts

Quickly create or access financial transactions:

- **Ctrl + Alt + W**: Write a check.
- **Ctrl + Alt + D**: Deposit funds.
- **Ctrl + Alt + T**: Track time for employees or projects.
- **Ctrl + Alt + V**: Enter vendor bills.

2.3. Data Management Shortcuts

Simplify data entry and modification:

- **Tab**: Move to the next field.
- **Shift + Tab**: Move to the previous field.
- **Ctrl + Enter**: Save a form or transaction.
- **Esc**: Close a window or cancel an action.

2.4. Date Shortcuts

Effortlessly enter dates in QuickBooks Online:

- **T**: Enter today's date.
- **Y**: Enter the first day of the year.
- **R**: Enter the last day of the year.
- **M**: Enter the first day of the month.
- **H**: Enter the last day of the month.
- **+ or -**: Increment or decrement the date by one day.

3. How to Master Keyboard Shortcuts

3.1. Start with Frequently Used Shortcuts

Identify the actions you perform most often in QuickBooks Online and focus on learning the shortcuts for those tasks first.

3.2. Use Quick Reference Guides

Create or download a printable list of keyboard shortcuts and keep it near your workspace for quick access.

3.3. Practice Regularly

Incorporate shortcuts into your daily workflow. The more you use them, the more intuitive they'll become.

3.4. Customize Your Workflow

While QuickBooks Online doesn't allow for custom keyboard shortcuts, you can adapt your workflow to make the most of the available options. For example:

- Memorize shortcuts for recurring tasks like creating invoices or entering expenses.
- Use the date shortcuts when entering transactions to speed up data entry.

4. Time-Saving Scenarios with Keyboard Shortcuts

Keyboard shortcuts shine in various scenarios, particularly when dealing with repetitive tasks or high-volume data entry.

4.1. Creating Invoices

- Shortcut: **Ctrl + Alt + I**
- Use case: Open a new invoice window instantly to create and send invoices faster.

4.2. Managing Expenses

- Shortcut: **Ctrl + Alt + E**
- Use case: Quickly record expenses, categorize them, and save the transaction with **Ctrl + Enter**.

4.3. Navigating Reports

- Shortcut: **Ctrl + Alt + R**
- Use case: Access financial reports directly to analyze performance without navigating through multiple menus.

4.4. Entering Dates

- Shortcut: Use **T**, **Y**, **R**, **M**, **H**, and **+/-**
- Use case: Enter transaction dates quickly without manually scrolling through a calendar.

5. Tips for Integrating Shortcuts into Your Workflow

5.1. Identify High-Impact Areas

Focus on shortcuts for tasks that take up the majority of your time, such as invoicing, reconciling accounts, or generating reports.

5.2. Train Your Team

Share a list of shortcuts with your team and encourage them to incorporate these into their workflows.

5.3. Use Shortcuts with Other Efficiency Tools

Combine keyboard shortcuts with QuickBooks Online features like automation rules, recurring transactions, and saved customizations to maximize productivity.

5.4. Regularly Revisit Shortcuts

QuickBooks Online periodically updates its features. Check the **Ctrl + Alt +?** menu to stay informed about new shortcuts.

6. Overcoming Challenges with Keyboard Shortcuts

6.1. Remembering Multiple Shortcuts

- **Solution**: Focus on a few shortcuts at a time and gradually expand your knowledge.

6.2. Difficulty in Multi-User Environments

- **Solution**: Encourage team-wide adoption to ensure consistency and efficiency.

6.3. Incompatibility with Older Systems

- **Solution**: Ensure your browser and QuickBooks Online are updated to the latest versions to support all shortcuts.

7. The Impact of Keyboard Shortcuts on Productivity

Keyboard shortcuts can have a profound impact on your productivity:

- Reduce the time spent on repetitive tasks by up to 50%.
- Minimize errors by providing direct access to tools and features.
- Enhance workflow consistency, especially in team settings where multiple users interact with QuickBooks Online.

8. Looking Ahead: Evolving Your Efficiency

Mastering keyboard shortcuts is an excellent starting point for optimizing your workflow. To continue improving efficiency:

- Explore integrations that automate repetitive tasks, such as payment processing or inventory tracking.
- Use QuickBooks Online's customizable reports and dashboards to gain deeper insights with minimal effort.
- Stay updated on new features and shortcuts introduced in QuickBooks Online to maintain a competitive edge.

Keyboard shortcuts are a simple yet powerful way to accelerate your workflow in QuickBooks Online. By mastering these time-saving tools, you can navigate the platform effortlessly, complete routine tasks faster, and focus on strategic aspects of your business. Whether you're a business owner, accountant, or team member, incorporating keyboard shortcuts into your daily routine is a step toward greater efficiency and productivity.

With your newfound shortcut skills, you're ready to pair these efficiencies with other advanced features to maximize the value of QuickBooks Online for your business. Let's continue exploring ways to enhance your financial management processes!

Best Practices for Organized Bookkeeping: Staying Audit-Ready

Assets	This Year	Last Year
Current assets		
Cash and cash equivalents	$ 10,000	$ 10,000
Accounts receivable	35,000	30,000
Inventory	25,000	20,000
Total current assets	**70,000**	**60,000**
Fixed assets		
Plants and machinery	$ 20,000	$ 20,000
Less decreciation	-12,000	-10,000
Land	8,000	8,000
Intangible assets	2,000	1,500
Total assets	**88,000**	**79,500**

=

Liabilities and Shareholders' Equity		
Liabilities		
Accounts payable	$ 20,000	$ 15,000
Taxes payable	5,000	4,500
Long-term bonds issued	15,000	10,000
Total liabilities	**40,000**	**29,500**

+

Shareholder's equity		
Common stock	$ 40,000	$ 40,000
Retained earnings	8,000	10,000
Total shareholder's equity	**48,000**	**50,000**

=

Liabilities and shareholders' equity	$ 88,000	$ 79,500

intuit quickbooks.

Organized bookkeeping is essential for running a successful business. It provides the foundation for accurate financial reporting, helps track performance, and ensures compliance with tax regulations. Beyond day-to-day management, staying audit-ready requires a systematic approach to maintaining clean, consistent, and well-documented records. QuickBooks Online is a powerful tool that can simplify this process, but its effectiveness depends on how well you implement best practices.

In this chapter, we'll explore practical strategies for organized bookkeeping that keep your financial data accurate, accessible, and audit-ready.

1. Why Organized Bookkeeping Matters

Proper bookkeeping is more than just a legal requirement; it's a business necessity. Organized financial records provide insights into your business's health, support decision-making, and protect against potential penalties during audits.

1.1. Benefits of Organized Bookkeeping

- **Financial Clarity**: Track income, expenses, and cash flow accurately.
- **Tax Compliance**: Ensure records align with local, state, and federal tax requirements.
- **Audit Preparedness**: Minimize disruptions and penalties during audits.
- **Better Decision-Making**: Use reliable data to inform growth strategies.

1.2. Risks of Poor Bookkeeping

- Inaccurate records can lead to missed deductions or over-payment of taxes.
- Disorganized data may delay decision-making or create compliance risks.
- Inadequate documentation increases vulnerability during audits.

2. Setting Up a Solid Bookkeeping System

The foundation of organized bookkeeping begins with setting up a structured system in QuickBooks Online.

2.1. Customize Your Chart of Accounts

- Use a well-organized **Chart of Accounts** to categorize transactions.
- Tailor categories to match your business's needs, such as separating income streams or expense types.

2.2. Establish Consistent Data Entry Practices

- Record transactions in real time to ensure accuracy.
- Use automation tools like bank feeds to reduce manual data entry errors.

2.3. Implement Role-Based Access

- Assign user roles in QuickBooks Online to ensure that only authorized personnel have access to sensitive financial data.

2.4. Set Up Recurring Transactions

- Automate regular expenses or income entries, such as rent, subscriptions, or recurring invoices.

3. Maintaining Accurate Records

Accuracy is at the heart of organized bookkeeping. Small mistakes can snowball into significant issues over time.

3.1. Regular Reconciliations

- **Bank and Credit Card Reconciliation**:
- Match bank statements and credit card records with QuickBooks Online transactions at least monthly.
- Address discrepancies immediately to ensure alignment.

3.2. Keep Receipts and Documentation

- Attach digital copies of receipts, invoices, and contracts to corresponding transactions in QuickBooks Online.
- Use mobile apps to capture and upload receipts in real time.

3.3. Categorize Transactions Correctly

- Assign income and expenses to appropriate accounts.
- Use classes or tags in QuickBooks Online to track transactions by project, department, or location.

3.4. Avoid Duplicate Entries

- Review records regularly to identify and eliminate duplicate transactions.

4. Staying Tax-Ready

Taxes are a major part of bookkeeping, and preparation throughout the year ensures a smoother tax season.

4.1. Track Tax-Deductible Expenses

- Categorize deductible expenses, such as office supplies, travel, and equipment, accurately.
- Maintain documentation for all deductions in case of an audit.

4.2. Automate Tax Calculations

- Use QuickBooks Online's tax features to calculate and track sales tax, payroll tax, and estimated tax payments.

4.3. Generate Tax Reports

- Use QuickBooks Online's **Profit and Loss Statement**, **Balance Sheet**, and **Tax Liability Report** to prepare for filing.

4.4. Plan for Estimated Taxes

- Set aside funds for quarterly estimated tax payments to avoid penalties.

5. Leveraging Automation for Efficiency

Automation reduces manual effort and enhances accuracy, making it a cornerstone of modern bookkeeping.

5.1. Sync Bank Feeds

- Connect your bank and credit card accounts to QuickBooks Online for real-time transaction updates.

5.2. Use Rules for Categorization

- Create rules in QuickBooks Online to automatically categorize transactions based on criteria like vendor names or amounts.

5.3. Schedule Recurring Reports

- Automate the generation of monthly or quarterly financial reports to monitor performance.

5.4. Integrate Third-Party Tools

- Use integrations like Receipt Bank or Hubdoc to streamline receipt management and data entry.

6. Staying Audit-Ready

Audits can be stressful, but organized records and preparation can make the process straightforward.

6.1. Maintain an Audit Trail

- Use QuickBooks Online's **Audit Log** to track changes to financial data, such as edits to invoices or deleted transactions.

6.2. Organize Supporting Documents

- Store contracts, tax forms, and receipts digitally within QuickBooks Online or in secure cloud storage.

6.3. Conduct Internal Reviews

- Periodically review financial records to ensure they are accurate and compliant with regulations.

6.4. Retain Records for the Required Period

- Keep financial records, including tax filings and payroll data, for the duration required by law (typically 3–7 years).

7. Best Practices for Ongoing Bookkeeping

To maintain organized records over time, adopt these best practices:

7.1. Schedule Regular Bookkeeping Time

- Dedicate time weekly or monthly to review and update financial records.

7.2. Separate Business and Personal Finances

- Use a dedicated business bank account and credit card to prevent mingling personal and business transactions.

7.3. Review Key Financial Metrics

- Monitor metrics like cash flow, profit margins, and accounts receivable aging regularly to stay informed.

7.4. Work with a Professional

- Collaborate with an accountant or bookkeeper for complex tasks or to review your records periodically.

8. Common Bookkeeping Mistakes and How to Avoid Them

Despite best efforts, bookkeeping mistakes can happen. Here's how to address common errors:

8.1. Misclassifying Transactions

- **Problem**: Assigning transactions to incorrect categories.
- **Solution**: Use QuickBooks Online's tools to review and reclassify transactions.

8.2. Ignoring Reconciliations

- **Problem**: Skipping reconciliations leads to mismatched accounts.
- **Solution**: Reconcile accounts monthly to catch errors early.

8.3. Forgetting to Back Up Data

- **Problem**: Losing financial records due to technical failures.
- **Solution**: Use QuickBooks Online's cloud storage and create additional backups if needed.

9. The Role of QuickBooks Online in Organized Bookkeeping

QuickBooks Online offers a range of features to simplify bookkeeping:

- **Automation**: Streamline data entry, categorization, and reporting.
- **Integration**: Connect with tools for time tracking, receipt management, and payroll.
- **Customization**: Tailor reports and dashboards to focus on the data that matters most.
- **Accessibility**: Access financial records from anywhere with secure cloud storage.

10. Benefits of Organized Bookkeeping

The rewards of maintaining organized financial records extend beyond compliance:

- **Confidence in Data**: Rely on accurate records for decision-making.
- **Stress-Free Audits**: Present clean, well-documented records to auditors or tax authorities.
- **Improved Cash Flow**: Monitor and manage cash flow effectively.
- **Scalability**: Lay a strong foundation for growth as your business expands.

Organized bookkeeping is a vital practice that supports financial stability, compliance, and growth. By implementing the strategies and best practices outlined in this chapter, you can maintain clean, accurate records that are always audit-ready. QuickBooks Online's tools and features provide the structure and automation needed to streamline your bookkeeping processes, leaving you free to focus on growing your business.

With a solid system in place, you're prepared to tackle financial challenges, seize opportunities, and navigate audits with ease. Let's continue exploring how QuickBooks Online can help you build a robust foundation for long-term success!

CONCLUSION

Throughout this guide, we have explored the depth and breadth of QuickBooks Online, unraveling its features to simplify the complexities of financial management. From the foundational steps of account setup to the advanced tools for customization, reporting, and troubleshooting, this journey has equipped you with the knowledge and skills needed to harness the full potential of this platform.

QuickBooks Online is not just a tool for managing your business finances; it is a cornerstone for efficiency, accuracy, and informed decision-making. Each chapter has built on the last, creating a comprehensive framework that you can rely on to streamline your processes, save time, and improve overall financial health.

The practices and strategies discussed in this guide are not merely theoretical—they are actionable and practical steps that, when implemented, transform the way you manage your business. Whether you're tracking inventory, preparing for tax season, or analyzing reports to plan for growth, the methods laid out here are designed to ensure precision and efficiency.

The ultimate goal of mastering QuickBooks Online is empowerment. It's about giving you the tools and confidence to stay on top of your finances, navigate challenges, and seize opportunities. By adopting the practices outlined here, you're not just managing your business—you're preparing it for success, scalability, and resilience.

As you move forward, continue to apply what you've learned. Use the insights gained to refine your processes, embrace innovation, and approach financial management with clarity and confidence. QuickBooks Online has the power to adapt and grow with your business, and with your newfound mastery, so do you. This is not the end of your journey—it is the beginning of a more organized, efficient, and successful way of managing your business's financial future.

www.ingramcontent.com/pod-product-compliance
Lightning Source LLC
Chambersburg PA
CBHW071412050326
40689CB00010B/1845